Mastering Uncertainty

The 3 Strategies You Need To Know

Keith Bickel, PhD

STRATEGY PRESS

Published by Strategy Press, Washington, D.C.

Library of Congress Cataloging-in-Publication Data:

Bickel, Keith.
Mastering Uncertainty: The 3 Strategies You Need To Know /
Keith Bickel.
p. cm.
ISBN 978-0-578-09399-4
1. Business Strategy. 2. Management & Leadership. 3. Business & Economics.

For Andrew Marshall

Mentor extraordinaire
And master of the tonal inflection
in one word – "right"

For my Family

My wonderful wife, Suzan
And my two biggest joys, JK and JM

CONTENTS

CONTENTS

PREFACE

Now more than ever, corporations big and small face economic and market uncertainty created by inconsistent government economic and financial policy, unknown and unexpected competitors, rapid technological changes, and more. So how do you plan for the future without knowing what the market environment will be or what inadvertent changes government policies and regulation will cause? How do you craft a strategy to position yourself for a competition you know will emerge, but about which little is known or even knowable for some time? How do you prepare for the upheaval that technological changes – particularly new web business models – will cause among both markets and competitors? Quite simply, in the absence of vision and feedback, how do you lead?

Well, the latest rage in management strategy is to advise those of you facing uncertainty to innovate, innovate, innovate. The problem is, if you read all that advice carefully, you discover the first paradox – that you need a vision to guide the innovation. But isn't the essence of uncertainty the fact that there is no easy formation of a vision? Indeed, there are painful penalties for producing the wrong vision. Then there is the paradox of innovation – innovation itself can create uncertainty, like all the financial innovation that nearly caused another Great Depression.

If the answer were as easy as innovation there wouldn't be so many firms facing uncertainty. It requires a lot more thought. Leaders facing periods of uncertainty cannot form (some would say cannot risk forming) a simplistic focus on innovation. Not that you shouldn't innovate. But the point of uncertainty is that you don't know in which direction to innovate. Yet you still have a need to prepare for a market you know is changing and to beat a competition you know will emerge. And that is what this book is about – preparing you for the task ahead – facing the uncertainty and learning how to master it.

1 UNCERTAINTY AND ADVANTAGE

What do we mean by uncertainty? True uncertainty means not knowing what is occurring or will occur in the external environment around you and how to react to it – to the point of not even knowing how to think about the future. This is not the uncertainty of whether a market will grow by 5% or 10% next year. Nor is it the uncertainty of day-to-day questions of who or where the next customer is coming from, or how much revenue and profit will you earn. Every business faces that kind of tactical uncertainty – the normal, practical realities related to running any successful business. No, the type of uncertainty that this book addresses is more strategic and more threatening – the uncertainty of whether there will even be a market next year, or whether your firm will even be in existence next year.

The sources of such uncertainty can be multiple. Uncertainty may arise from the structure of the marketplace. For example, no one can size the market; size component market segments; figure out how to segment the market; determine what products or services are desired; or create appropriate distribution channels for reaching unknown potential customers. Uncertainty may arise from the supply side as well. No one can know what technology will be required to make as yet unknown products; what processes will be required; or even what business model is required to sustain revenues. Uncertainty may arise from external business uncertainty. New players may suddenly swarm into a marketplace. There may be sudden government regulation or intervention in the market. Competing services may spring up suddenly. Your firm's own market movement can even generate uncertainty. If your firm ventures beyond its traditional markets and experiments with new business models, you may find yourself among other firms pursuing very different competitive strategies. The result can be heightened competition and dramatically increased uncertainty on all fronts.

Such uncertainty invites ill-conceived behaviors such as sticking ones head in the sand and doing nothing. That's where this book will help you. If you want to master uncertainty, you need an effective strategy to do so. Why do you need a strategy when you could always just try to wait out the uncertainty – when you could let others take the risk of moving, of investing, while you sit back and watch? Well, the answer goes back to the type of uncertainty this book is designed to help you master. It's the type of uncertainty that kills off firms – whether you are in a bubble (Bear, Lehman), technology is shifting rapidly (Kodak, Palm), new business models are emerging (Blockbuster, print media), and more. And if you wait for the uncertainty to resolve, by that time it is too late to start thinking about your firm's survival. It's the type of uncertainty that creates paradoxes you may not even realize. You may think you are taking lower risk by simply waiting when in fact you are taking the greater risk of failure when certainty arrives. You may think the price of investing in a strategy is too high when in fact the price to be paid for doing nothing is far higher. So if you don't want to incur the high risk or high price of failure, you need a strategy.

If you need a strategy, the first question then becomes: a strategy towards what goal when all is uncertain. This is where the concept of competitive advantage comes into play. Achieving one or more advantages becomes the key goal of the strategy you pick, because focusing on that will give you the flexibility you need to deal with the uncertainty you face. Understanding it is central to following the logic of the strategies that are discussed in the following chapters. This is because your views on advantage will inevitably play a large role in which strategy or strategies you pursue.

Accordingly, the rest of this chapter focuses on competitive advantage so that you understand goal setting in the context of crafting each of the strategies that follow. Feel free, however, to skip ahead to any of the strategy chapters and then refer back to this one as needed. Doing so might even provide additional context around what to aim for once you've got a sense of how you might want to deal with the uncertainty you face.

What Is Competitive Advantage?

Competitive advantage exists when you develop the ability to impose your will on marketplace competitors. When you can deter, dissuade or block competitors from taking certain actions, you've got it. When you can defend against competitor actions, you've also got it. Competitive advantage can even be used to defeat competitors outright, as WordPerfect did when it drove Wang, WordStar, XYWrite, and others from the word processing market in the 1980's.

By understanding advantage as a competitive force, we don't have to limit ourselves to discussions of corporations. We can also talk about "mission-maximizing" entities like charities and government agencies. We don't often think about charities as competitive institutions, but indeed they are (they compete for your dollars don't they?). And so, advantage can be discussed in a way that applies to these entities as well. In their case, advantage is demonstrated when they have the ability to conduct activities at a particular point in time or within a given timeframe. For example, a charity like the Red Cross survives because it has the competitive ability (in this case, branding and fundraising) to create donation surges that enable it to deliver disaster relief successfully. It also has the infrastructure to deliver on those donations. Compared to profit-making enterprises it may appear to have low-to-no-"profits." But what it has is sustainability.

This point on sustainability is an important one because it comprises one of the two key frames through which competitive advantage is often viewed. The other frame is profitability. Most corporate, charity, and government leaders viscerally understand this dual conception and tend to talk at this level of abstraction. Make money or stay alive: that's the name of the game. What the level of abstraction hides, though, are some subtle complexities brought about by the competitive nature of the environment. Those complexities in turn suggest that the two frames are misleading indicators of the presence of real advantage.

For example, in the case of profitability, most research tends to define it in relative terms – often as better profits compared to competitors. Despite the allure of simplicity, this approach doesn't work so well. Most firms – yours included – generally cannot generate profits above their competitors for more than several years. Meanwhile, which type of profit are we looking for? Is it gross profit? Net profit? Earnings before taxes, depreciation, and amortization (EBITDA)? Most industry leaders form different views of profit depending on the accounting conventions that affect them most. There is a potential trap here, however. With various industries (particularly technology) tending toward convergence, there may be new competitors that go unnoticed. Who would have suspected Apple would become a market leader in selling songs? What this means is that you have to become familiar with the conventions of profitability among the sectors that potentially adjoin your own. You want to avoid the strategic surprise caused by a firm that would be considered marginally profitable by one convention suddenly looking like a powerful competitor when it breaks into your market.

Using profitability to determine advantage is further undermined by the problem of time spans. Quarter to quarter profits aren't worth paying attention to, except to follow trends for seasonality or growth and decline. Generally speaking, research on profit-seeking advantage tends to focus on a 5-20 year horizon. The outer part of that time span may seem a bit long in some industries. For technology start-ups, a decade may seem like an interminably long time. For more established firms, though, twenty years may be viewed as a better measure to encompass their going through at least two economic cycles.

Turning from profitability to survivability, the later turns out to be only a marginally better frame for demonstrating the presence of advantage. For example, non-profit entities are not the only ones to have a timeframe or milestone focus. Two types of corporations may also have a similar focus. One is a business trying to sell itself. In this case, the CEO of a business for sale will usually seek rapid if somewhat temporary marketplace growth to boost profits and influence negotiations. Does that firm have an advantage, or is it making disadvantageous sacrifices? The other case is a business like a biotechnology firm, heavily engaged in research and development in order to develop a novel drug or medical device. Profitability may well be negative (by any measure) for a long time with the possibility of a sudden revenue explosion. Here, advantage will not be visible to someone overly focused on profits, but obvious to someone focused on competitive behavior.

The Underlying Basis for Advantage: Time, Structure or Resources

Advantage as a concept is rarely discussed inside the corporation. In your firm, probably a handful of individuals, at best, can articulate what the competitive advantages necessary for success are. Indeed, they often cannot even articulate what the underlying bases for your advantages are. Without understanding those bases, you can utterly miss how competitors can re-conceptualize how they compete against you, or how you can turn the tables on them. So, what are the underlying bases of advantage?

There are three fundamental underlying bases for any given advantage in your industry. One basis is time, as in competing by leveraging time in some manner to build advantages or compete better. Another basis is structure, as in the structure of the market(s) in which you operate may dictate which advantage(s) you can realistically seek. The final underlying basis is resources, as in the resources you can access (natural and otherwise) will dictate what kinds of advantages you can seek. What you will find as you continue reading is that the first and third –

time and resources – form the most logical bases you can leverage to develop advantage. As such you will see them referenced more than once in the chapters to follow.

Taking time first, the signs of competitive advantage are usually associated with very short-term phenomenon. A key concept here is hyper-competition, an old concept that rose to prominence during the 1980's and again during the tech boom of the 1990's. The premise of hyper-competition is that companies achieving it keep their competitors off their feet or away from their strengths by competing to be faster. The overarching goal is to be the first to market or to grab the larger market share.

According to fans of hyper-competition, moving faster conveys advantage no matter how temporary. Competition becomes a "war of movement." Success depends on developing quick responses to market events. The essence of strategy becomes not how you structure your firm's products and bring them to market but how you time the dynamics of your behavior. Companies seek to be able to execute fast, aggressive, and intelligent actions that confuse competitors. Modularity, or slicing up processes into discrete components, often becomes important here. So does seemingly unconnected resource investment; investing in both product development and unrelated alternatives adds surprise, flexibility, and unpredictability to a firm's activities. The idea is to make the link between investment and market disruptions appear disconnected rather than linear. Your competitors can't read your financials or see your product releases and find trends that might hint of future intents.

While the concept of time-based competition clearly has its place in terms of understanding advantage, you have to be careful not to make too much of it. Recall from above that competing on time was a "big idea" of the 1980's. Well, when researchers went back to study companies that professed to compete based on time to market, they found that those companies had developed alternative competencies as well. They had improved the quality of their products compared to competitors. They had developed customer insights or other intangible capabilities that allowed them to exploit markets. They had entered new businesses or innovated and produced new ideas within their own industry. The upshot, at least looking at an earlier generation of speed-competing companies, is that time may not have been the true basis for their competitive advantage but rather an enabler of the other capabilities that then allowed those firms to compete more successfully.

The notion of hyper-competition that re-emerged in the 1990's with the internet avoided the idea of head-to-head competition. The new idea was to move away from or stay ahead of the competition. Firms could do this by moving to new products that re-defined the competitive market. Or, they could move to new pricing models that competitors were unable to emulate (e.g., advertising for online greeting card stores). Or, they could develop new distribution models that avoided competitor's strengths (e.g., Peapod for grocery delivery).

If hyper-competition sounds like it was re-incarnated in the 1990's as a guide for internet entrepreneurs, most of whom died off, that does not mean the advice was all bad. In fact, there is still much that makes sense for a small firm seeking to compete in an old market. Be flexible and give way when attacked directly by a superior force. Avoid directly taking on established competitors that are bigger and stronger (i.e., avoid sumo matches). Acknowledge what competitors are doing right, then copy and extend their smart moves faster than they can. Exploit the slower bureaucracy of established competitors to offer their customers faster service. Build alliances with those threatened by your competition's success (or as they say in diplomacy: the enemy of my enemy is my friend).

While hyper-competition holds some appeal as a way to build advantage, especially for start-ups, it has some serious drawbacks as well. Competing on time requires a level of continuous market and competitor insight that is rare in the real world. An unstated assumption is that you can operate constantly inside the time horizons of your competitors. Let's assume for the moment that this can happen. Let's further assume this occurs because all other firms learn and innovate slower than your firm. That still doesn't give your firm the advantage you might think. Differences between firms matter. Your competitors all innovate at different speeds from each other and from you, for that matter. This means they are likely to fire innovations at the market at different intervals. In the aggregate they could wind up firing innovations at the market far faster than your ability to cope, leaving you unable to shape the market as much as the hyper-competition model would suggest. You may have a difficult time enough as it is just being in response mode.

A second problem with time-based competition is that at some point you have to take a stand and establish some permanence or risk running right out of markets and consequently out of business. Business scholars who know little about guerrilla warfare are enamored with the concept of firms making a strike and then running away. Well, when that happens, eventually one of two outcomes result. The lack of continuity causes customers to migrate to your more consistent competitors. Or, you run out of innovative juice and fall back into competitive rhythms set by others, at which point you risk getting squashed by firms relying on advantages outside of your strengths.

And just what might the bases of their advantages be if not time-based? Here, the other two underlying bases – structure and resources – come to the fore.

The structural school says that a firm's competitive strategies are dependent on whether its market scope is narrow or wide. Where market scope is narrow (e.g., mortgage securitization), you would likely seek advantage by becoming the lowest cost, most efficient producer. Where market scope is wide, (e.g., auto sales), you would seek advantage by differentiating from your competitors. You would not need to be low-cost, and in fact might not want to be. You could choose to pursue a high-cost strategy if you opted to be a luxury brand, as Ferrari does. The problem occurs when you fail to choose decisively between basing advantage on cost or differentiation. Then you risk becoming "stuck in the middle," as has become the case with some car manufacturers (e.g., Mercedes Benz).

Like the hyper-competition school of thought, the structuralist school has both earlier and later versions. The more recent variant argues that the geographic structure of industry – where firms are located or clustered like along the I-270 "bio-tech corridor" outside Washington D.C. – helps explain competitive advantage. Advantage in this situation is developed because the network of competing firms is able to draw on a common nearby talent pool, or to build a talent pool through a local university (think Silicon Valley and Stanford) that is not as readily accessible to competitors in other geographic areas. Alternatively, advantage can be gained because the central location of competitors draws more customers (almost as a destination site) than one firm alone could on its own. The existence of Chinatown and Little Italy in many cities illustrates this idea perfectly.

Finally, the last underlying basis of advantage is the resource base available to the firm. This is often referred to as the "resource based view" (or RBV) school of thought. Proponents of RBV argue that clustering by itself (as in the example above) would not confer advantage but rather gives rise to it through other means. Those other means could be the accumulation of resources, assets, capabilities, and / or competencies that are valuable, rare, inimitable or non-substitutable (or VRIN in strategy parlance). RBV adherents believe that firms that develop some key resource or capability that is either valuable, rare, inimitable, or non- substitutable can then be leveraged to create a firm's competitive advantage.

Note that this is not a product-centric view of competency building. RBV proponents assume (correctly for the most part) that products can easily be reverse engineered and ultimately imitated. Instead, they argue that competency building should be based on more ambiguous resources (say, a particularly difficult process) so that it is less susceptible to duplication. The risk, of course, is that if the link between a particular advantage and success is ambiguous to competitors, the link may be similarly ambiguous to internal management. A great example of this is the case study of a highly successful laundry delivery service where the key advantage lay in the drivers' relationships with the customers, and the firm did not know this until an outside researcher figured it out. How ironic to develop a recipe for success and not even know it, which of course raises the risk that it cannot be leveraged or sustained.

The Layers of Advantage

Apart from the underlying bases of advantage, separately you need to think about four layers of advantage that can exist in a firm: in resources, assets, capabilities or competencies. These four are often thought of together in a hierarchy of advantage. The utility of them is that they not only build from the concrete to the conceptual, they can bundle and nest in the next higher level. Resources can bundle to become assets. Assets can bundle to become capabilities. Capabilities can bundle to become competencies.

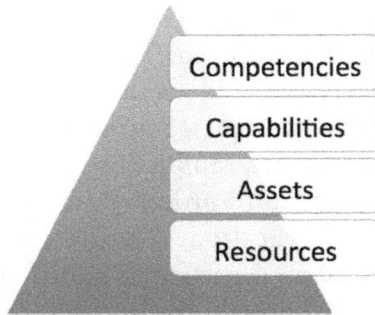

Starting from the bottom, resources can be viewed three different ways: as inputs (both raw and finished), as time, and as tangible items (e.g., specialty equipment, expertise). Resources can then be combined or bundled to produce tangible and intangible assets. Note that in moving from the concrete to the more conceptual, the notion of tangible also changes. For example, human capital may now be considered tangible in context, such as having a particular chemistry expertise. Organizations may now be considered tangible, such as having a superior sales force. While the knowledge embodied in that sales force may be intangible, the unit itself (and its capabilities) are very tangible to the firm. On the intangible side, assets might be reputation, buyer-supplier relations, and process expertise.

At the next layer of advantage, capabilities involve the ability to integrate resources and assets to generate new value-creation opportunities. An example might involve integrating product development with market intelligence. Other capabilities might involve re-configuring resources in the firm, such as creating new processes for manufacturing replication. Firms in the knowledge management space may create capabilities around copying, transferring, and recombining information products to leverage work done for prior customers. The consulting group McKinsey tends to be very good at this. In addition to integrating or reconfiguring resources, capabilities may involve re-allocating them. The ability to move resources from hub to spoke and back again rapidly is an example. Just-in-time delivery is a related example. The ability to patch, split, and recombine entire business units to keep up with shifting market demand exemplifies yet another capability set. A perfect example of this is PC maker Dell's constant re-segmentation of business lines to align with customer desires.

Developing capabilities can also entail building new routines. Routines may be devised around the ways companies manage time, such as during the production cycle, during change management, and sales and distribution timing, to name a few. Note that owning a hard asset, or having a certain infrastructure generally is not a capability so much as a proxy for the capability. For example, if a firm has just-in-time (JIT) delivery capability, then owning the trucks is not the capability; knowing how to execute is the capability.

If capabilities involve combinations of assets, then capabilities too can be combined to create a fourth level of advantage – competencies. Casio, for example, integrated its capabilities in miniaturization, microprocessor design, material science, ultra-thin precision casing to create miniature radios. Note that radio production was not the actual competency; the ability to make miniature ones was. Competencies may also involve how capabilities are organized to deliver value to the customer. Citicorp, for example, combined workflows (capability) with information systems (another capability) in a way that allowed it to pioneer participating in world financial markets 24 hours a day (a key competency in this case leading to an early advantage).

When thinking about competencies, a key mistake to avoid is assuming that a firm's competency is what they do better than the other things that they do. Not so. The competence is what they do better than anyone else. That makes competencies a lot harder to benchmark, but doing so is critical. When measured and done well, building and even combining competencies can lead to either deeper or wider market penetration. An example is 3M's sticky tape. 3M had over time developed competencies in areas such as substrates, coatings, and adhesives that were used in a variety of products. In turn, those competencies had been built from product capabilities involving magnetic tape, photo film, pressure-sensitive tapes, and coated abrasives. The scientist who made the initial sticky tape discovery did so leveraging knowledge developed across competencies. The result was a new product that in turn led to whole new markets that had not previously existed. In sum, 3M's initial business lines gave rise to competencies (non-permanent adhesives in particular) that in turn led to new business lines that 3M could dominate behind the protective wall of patents.

While 3M could hide behind patents, corporations in service-related industries generally cannot build barriers around their intellectual capital. This is where the Resource Based View (RBV) concept of ambiguity discussed above can be important. Specifically, two types of ambiguity can be helpful in hiding advantages from competitors. One is linkage ambiguity. This occurs when outsiders do not realize a linkage exists between a competency and potential advantage you have developed. The other ambiguity is characteristic ambiguity. This occurs when the competency is not well understood in and of itself, such as when the competency arises from a firm's organizational culture or values.

Note that ambiguity can be a very good thing from your perspective. So long as you understand the competency that resides inside your firm, then from a competitive standpoint you should appreciate ambiguity. Ambiguity leaves your competitors scratching their heads as to the sources of your success. The catch is not to confuse yourself, too. If ambiguity is too high early on, and your own workforce becomes confused about the sources of your potential success, then you won't get the kinds of experimentation that can generate market success. For example, in 3M's case, its scientists understood the firm's competencies in glues and substrates, and from that could experiment with how to marry the two in innovative ways that led to break-out products.

In the final analysis, there are three ways to think about ambiguity from a practical point of view. If a competency is easy to imitate, then you should strive to increase ambiguity so that your competitors cannot figure out which competency they should imitate. If a competency is not easy to imitate then you should strive to reduce ambiguity as much possible so that your firm can leverage its human capital more effectively. Finally, if you need to change a significant portion of your management team, then reduce ambiguity as much as possible during and somewhat after the transition period. Otherwise, you risk your new managers accidentally eliminating a competency you actually need.

Can Advantage Be Measured?

Figuring out which competencies to keep and which to divest requires you to determine how much advantage you gain from them. Imagine how difficult this task is under the conditions of market uncertainty posited at the beginning of this chapter. The RBV school (mentioned earlier) suggests some measures – valuable, rare, inimitable, and non-substitutable.

The first measure of advantage, inimitability, is particularly useful because it applies broadly across industries and also within them. Patents are an example that applies across industries. No one in any industry is allowed to violate your patent. Real estate is an example that applies within industries. Competitors generally cannot own the same real estate, forcing the late-comer to seek alternatives. Imitation can also be thwarted by creating bottlenecks. An example of this is when a company locks up a vital commodity from a third world country, and uses (abuses) the political process to stymie entry of follow-on competitors. The competition knows the solution but simply cannot execute it.

A second measure of advantage is that of durability. How quickly does the basis for advantage (typically in this case an asset or resource) deteriorate? For example, if you attempt to build a software or technical advantage based on a technology whose lifespan is typically 3-4 years, you can expect swift erosion of any advantage. If, on the other hand, you build advantage based on being the fastest to market with upgrades then advantage can take on a much longer lifespan.

A third measure of advantage is whether value is generated by a particular resource or capability and whether the value / resource / capability can be moved. Value tied to a static resource, like geographic location, can generate advantage and do so durably. On the other hand, any resource or capability that is highly mobile is difficult to leverage for advantage unless it is layered into larger processes that are less mobile. This particularly applies to the services sector. If, say, an investment bank's value is tied up in people who can do deals, then the firm is at risk of those dealmakers walking out the door and setting up a competitor. If those same people are wedded to processes, units, or technology they cannot replicate without extreme expense, then the firm is more likely to achieve advantage from them over a longer time horizon.

A fourth measure of advantage is that of substitutability. This measure applies throughout the value chain from input to customer. Can a reasonable substitute be found that overcomes a competitor's advantage? For inputs, maybe there is a different resource that, while not quite in the same category, can still be used to generate profits. An example from the PC industry would be the use of USB memory sticks instead of drive media like floppies, CD ROMs, and DVDs. Substitutes need not be physical. They can be conceptual as well. For example, you may not be able to compete on price, but the complexity of the product or service you offer allows you to compete based on superior training and customer service. Alternatively, you could compete by having a superior return policy, the implied warranty of which draws customers from the lower cost competitors to you instead.

Can Advantage Be Maintained?

Unfortunately, being able to measure advantage over time does not mean that advantage itself is durable. Whether you can maintain the advantage depends on your time horizon and what the basis for advantage is in your particular industry. The longer the time horizon the less you should believe you can maintain the advantage. Even in the short term, advantage may not be maintainable if you or your competition engages in hyper-competition.

On the other hand, if market structures underpin advantage in your market, then you may be more likely to be able to maintain advantage over longer periods of time. This is because many markets generally evolve very slowly, probably even predictably, over long periods of time before rapid, short-term changes occur. These changes can produce disconcerting turmoil in the market before a new competitive balance is established. Then slow change becomes the norm again. During these slower periods, advantage by and large is maintainable. Note the implication here. Rarely is it in a firm's interest to create long-term volatility in the marketplace. Your firm may "shake things up" a bit based on your own strengths (e.g., consolidate the market rolling up smaller rivals). But you would not want to do so continuously.

The danger occurs, of course, when rival firms decide to take on the industry leader (you, hopefully) with game-changing strategies of their own. Those rivals can inadvertently create a fluid marketplace where the basis for advantage and competition changes too quickly for any one firm to emerge victorious. Equilibrium becomes difficult to establish, even though all the players' interests are aligned with reducing the rate of change. Practically speaking, you and your rivals wind up making sub-optimal decisions (because you cannot collude) that leaves everyone worse off than had they simply tried to take you on directly. How you stop this cascade once started is difficult to say. You may have to acquire the offending rival to stop it from driving the pace of change. This becomes a problem if that rival happens to be large – like Apple.

Sometimes your own behavior can be the stumbling block to maintaining advantages. Resource decisions are not always rationale. You may overlook or refuse to keep certain resources, skills, knowledge, or the like. There are three reasons why you might engage in such self-denial. First is the difficulty of altering entrenched organizational habits and routines. This is why new management is often hired to make necessary changes. Second is unfamiliarity; what is new is often unfamiliar and the unfamiliar usually causes fear and doubt. These emotions then cloud your ability to undertake necessary changes. Third is cultural mismatch; replacing entrenched values or practices can be perceived as inappropriate to your firm, or even disloyal to your firm's norms and values.

In short, sustaining advantage over the long-term is highly unrealistic. Markets are in a constant state of flux. And if not, then one or more competitors are motivated to make them so. Somebody always has a vested interest in upsetting any equilibrium that gets established. Additionally, normal behaviors and emotions involving habits, fear, and loyalty present formidable barriers to advantage-seeking behavior. Rather than a systematic assessment and choice of optimal resources, your management may engage in sub-optimal resource allocation and resistance to change.

2 FROM ADVANTAGE TO STRATEGY

Creating an advantage-centric strategy involves several trade-offs. The first is a trade-off between acting early in the hopes of swaying the outcome of the uncertainty, and acting later after the uncertainty is resolved. The second trade-off is between focusing investment on the most probable outcome and spreading investment around several possible outcomes. The strategies you will learn in the following chapters revolve around these two trade-offs.

By this point, you are probably realizing that if focus and time are key elements of coping with uncertainty, they are also the key elements for understanding advantage. It should come as no surprise then that the bases for strategy under uncertainty are the building of capabilities (on what to focus) and time-pacing.

Under capability-building, the role of strategy is to achieve one of two inter-related objectives. Either build or acquire abilities (assets, resources, capabilities and/or competencies) that are VRIN (valuable, rare, inimitable, and non-substitutable); or make otherwise common capabilities more VRIN.

Under time-pacing, the role of strategy is to differentiate yourself from the competition by how fast you operate. Unlike most other strategies, the key point here is not to become expert in one thing above all others because you risk being in the wrong place when uncertainty is resolved. Instead, you want to be deliberately, frequently and unpredictably different. What you are looking for (at least initially) are temporary advantages. Each advantage is a stepping-stone to the next set of changes you will implement. Don't try investing to defend these advantages either, because that would waste resources since they are only meant to be temporary anyway.

Under both bases of strategy – capabilities-based and time-pacing – there are a number of common-alities you should understand so that you can switch between strategic approaches as needed. The first commonality is a relentless focus on the future where you encourage and actively support improvisational planning techniques like scenario "gaming." Let your strategy team focus on creating those different futures. You should focus on what you need to build or acquire in order to meet those futures. Another commonality is the need to develop relationships outside your firm (or division). A good idea under uncertainty is to develop flexible relationships with counter-parties at different parts of the value chain – perhaps even more than you would ordinarily tolerate. Temporary alliances, joint ventures, and staff exchanges are examples of this approach. The point is that no one, no matter how creative, is likely to see all facets of uncertainty unfolding to resolution. Finally, another commonality is that improving performance in the marketplace is emphatically not about cutting costs. Indeed some form of inefficiency is embedded in the investment requirements of two of the strategies you will learn in the chapters to follow.

Turning from commonalities to differences, there are subtle (and sometimes not so subtle) differences between the bases for strategy that you should understand. Many of these differences are outright contradictions involving outlook and approach. The differences are important because your personal viewpoint will inevitably color the strategy you pick, and you should simply understand this and the impact it may have going forward.

One obvious difference is in the interpretation of market conditions. The unrestrained view of competition embedded in time-pacing is generally incompatible with capabilities-building. As you've learned already, time-pacing never wants an equilibrium. Continuous change is the goal; and your goal is to be the one creating that continuous change. By contrast, capabilities-building seeks to preserve advantage by reaching a new equilibrium, hopefully being first, but certainly with the right advantage(s) to dominate once that equilibrium is established.

Another, related difference between time-pacing and capabilities-building is in their conception of the source of competitive advantage and thus strategic purpose. Capabilities-building focuses on leveraging resources and competencies to achieve sustainable competitive advantage. Note the emphasis on longevity, another difference. Time-pacing focuses on apparently unrelated advantages, all short-lived. Even the mechanism of timing is different between the two. Capabilities-building measures time in terms of market and product lifecycles. Long-term planning horizons are thus desirable and feasible. Time-pacing measures time with a stopwatch. There are no natural cycles, no market cycles, no product cycles to which you should pay attention. Short-term, perhaps even rolling, planning is the norm.

Another difference between the two is the role of influence – the influence you gain in the process of achieving your desired objectives. Capabilities-building says that you gain influence by controlling key resources that in turn let you develop superior capabilities. These capabilities then give you influence to create sustainable competitive advantage and shape markets. Time-pacing says you gain influence from being seen as the one able to change the rules of the game. The drawback is that in order to maintain credibility you have to develop the ability to do so repetitively. Doing so once won't suffice and can dramatically reduce your influence.

Finally, capabilities-building and time-pacing disagree on the nature of relationships. For capabilities-building, you build relations with outside partners that will allow you to create or leverage particular advantage-rendering resources. The stickier the better so as to lock up resources and keep them away from competitors. Time-pacing, by contrast, sees sticky relationships as something to be avoided. Relationships are good so long as they are as dynamic as the pace at which you are driving your overall strategy. Thus, relationships will tend to be based more on short-term transactional considerations than, say, protecting particular advantages. It stands to reason that any relationship should be dissolvable at will, and that there is some impetus to do so regularly in order to create confusion and disadvantages for others (especially if that partner is a likely competitor).

From Two Drivers, Three Strategies

Up to this point, we've focused on two themes. The first is the centrality of focusing on advantage creation over other goals when faced with uncertainty. The second theme is to understand the two key drivers, capabilities-building and time-pacing. Now we turn our attention to the fun stuff; the three management strategies you need to know to master uncertainty. For ease of use, we will call them the pioneer, pouncer and hedging strategies.

Pioneer strategies are about building advantage to drive the resolution of uncertainty sooner rather than later. Note an underlying premise here; you must understand the uncertainty you face, at least well enough to shape its resolution. Pouncer strategies are concerned with building advantage to jump on and then move past the pioneer in the market to dominate it. Timing is critical. The pouncer starts later, so developing the ability to move faster than the pioneer becomes the primary aim of your strategy. Finally, hedging strategies, sometimes known as portfolio strategies, focus on the unforeseeable nature of the future (or the fallibility of human foresight, depending on your personal outlook) by developing a range of capabilities that position the firm to survive when the uncertainty is resolved. Since you may or may not use the capabilities you develop under a hedging strategy, what you are effectively developing are options. If you have not heard the term before, these are often called "real options" to distinguish them from equity options. (You will read more about these later in the chapter on hedging strategy.)

Most real options tend to be capabilities-based, hence the dominance of that driver in hedging strategies. At the same time, some options will be exercised earlier than others, giving you the opportunity to upset the market and shape some of the uncertainty. This suggests that time pacing can be wrapped around capabilities development, and vice versa. You will see how this can be so in the following chapters.

3 PIONEER STRATEGY

The goal of pioneer strategy is for you to develop an advantage or advantages that, even during uncertainty, allow you to beat your competition to market and establish dominance. You might develop pioneer strategies even when the gains are unclear. You might do this, for example, if you have a deep preference for one particular outcome and believe that you have the market strength to influence the resolution of uncertainty in your favor. However, you are bearing the risk of failure in terms of either guessing wrong on the outcome or your ability to influence that outcome.

Two core strategies can be leveraged to become a pioneer. One is time-pacing and the other is placing "big bets." Let's turn to each separately.

Time-Pacing Strategy

Time-pacing, as its name suggests, entails scheduling change at intervals you can predict, but your competition cannot. The point is to create some measure of certainty, or conversely to mitigate some of the unpredictability you face. Understand that, even with a fast tempo, time-pacing can create predictability. Paradoxically, letting your competition see your changes may be beneficial to you as the pioneer. Your competition may fall into the trap of thinking they have to compete the same way as you, forcing them to expend resources at a rate they ultimately cannot *sustain*.

Note the implied stopwatch aspect to this strategy. It is important to understand the subtle difference between chaotic and ordered change in the marketplace. Most people (and companies) pace themselves by events. They react to events and make changes accordingly. Each event tends to be treated as discreet or unique. Rarely do companies drive change to their own internal timeframe irrespective of what is happening elsewhere. Under the time-pacing strategy, this is in fact what you would do. You would drive the changes in the marketplace, forcing your competitors to pace themselves by events you create. If you are time-pacing, then your team(s) knows the internal timeframe (the clock, if you will) and thus by when they are supposed to accomplish what.

Time-pacing can be further refined into three sub-strategies. The first is driving the rate of change in the marketplace during the period of uncertainty. The second sub-strategy is developing the ability to see market behaviors sooner than the competition can. The third is simply moving first into a market space while not necessarily affecting the pace of change. In a sense, this last sub-strategy is a form of placing big bets, but in the timing sense.

For the first sub-strategy – driving the rate of change – to work, you need to excel at several tasks. You need to be able to discern "noise" from valid market or competitor signals and then be able to ignore the former. This is not always as easy it seems; you may have powerful peers who are helping create that "noise." You also need to be able to manage transitions well. The larger the firm the more difficult this becomes because the employee base will contain ever larger numbers of people averse to change. Tight strategic alignment down your chain of command is necessary. This is not to say your strategy needs to be conveyed in exquisite detail to all levels of the employee base. It may be enough to convey, set incentive benchmarks for, and create a culture around setting the clock against your competitors. Alignment as simple as that is often enough to provide change-averse employees with the security they need to understand that change is not threatening to their position, but rather strengthens it.

In addition to managing transitions, you also need to excel at managing rhythms. Rhythms may involve seasonality, customer spending habits, and press cycles (e.g., holiday gadget write-ups for gift ideas). The reason rhythms become so important is because they involve managing multiple transitions. You may be good at one major transition but not many of them one after the other. Being able to integrate multiple transitions is a key required skill for this strategy to work.

Transition integration also becomes key in a different dimension, that of managing alliances. Change pacing may sound great when applied against your competitors, but it fails miserably if you neglect to bring along key upstream and downstream partners. That is why this strategy often feels more appropriate for firms in the services industry or smaller firms that manufacture and retail their own products. A certain level of management expertise is required if a larger firm has to ensure its downstream value-added retailers (VARs) have appropriate shelf space, display paraphernalia, turnover cycles, and so forth. In some ways, if you have a large firm and can accomplish this kind of integration, as Microsoft and Dell seem to have, that could give you superior competitive positioning in the marketplace because your peer competition would have trouble accomplishing the same. Be aware that your smaller competitors may be able to compete, sharing in the benefits of your strategy. Just make sure that their success is not at your time and expense.

The second time-pacing strategy involves developing the ability to see market, and particularly customer, behaviors sooner than can your competitors. The chief utility of this strategy is seen in markets where consumer behavior is fickle, ill-understood, or simply unknown. The goal here is to develop and then leverage expertise in seeing the market better so you can be the first to market with new products, or even be the first to spot and enter an emerging market offshoot. Investment under this strategy all too often tends to be focused on information technology (IT). To do so is to miss investing in good people adept at spotting market trends that technology does not capture or that is captured in complex ways that still require human expertise to make sense. Nevertheless, the beauty of good IT investment is that it can link seemingly disparate parts of your firm to create a more complete picture of your customer behavior. Automating the collection and analysis of customer data allows you to realize time savings in your analytical cycle, as well as achieve more accuracy in your insights. If you can achieve those time cycles faster than your competition then you can more consistently be the first to market.

Finally, there is moving first as a simple competitive strategy. The point of this strategy almost seems the opposite of what has just been discussed above. Here, the premise is that market knowledge, because of time lags, offers a flawed picture on which to base market entry. Even so, market entry can be desirable as a way of clarifying the market picture. This is because, by leading, you impose a form of clarity by your actions. Here, the time-pacing is less about shortening internal cycles (like the preceding strategy) and more about driving your competitors to react to the external pace you are setting. One caveat is in order, however. This strategy often risks becoming a "build it and they will come" strategy. The great dot com bust of the early 2000's illustrated how dangerous this can be!

By now you may have noticed that time lags seem to be an embedded concept of the pioneer strategy. For example, there is the time lag it takes to observe competitor actions, and, there is the lag time reacting to those actions. These lags in turn can be exacerbated by inertia, particularly if the resulting change looks like it is largely irreversible. Irreversibility will alarm your management team and employees alike, slowing down the adoption of change. Time lags can also occur because your competitors' behavior is usually more difficult to discern than your customer behavior may be. While key competitor actions such as pricing can often be seen (even if murkily in some services sectors), many investment initiatives cannot. Information technology investment, for example, can be opaque to outside viewers. So can research and development, product prototyping, and the like. The risk is in a key competitor initiative going unobserved until implemented. At that point you have to move quickly to catch up. The problem is exacerbated if you cannot compress your activities to catch up, such as when a particular supplier gets locked up by contracts. You could be looking at years to overcome and respond appropriately in the market.

This last consideration – competitor behavior rather than customer behavior – should drive your pioneer strategy. You should aggressively try to set the agenda by beating your competitors to the market. You may do so confidently because you believe that you can achieve a duration advantage by moving first.

That is, you impose the lag problem on your competitors before they can impose it on you.

Big Bet Strategy

Where the other pioneer strategies have been about timing, this one is about focus. The concept of the big bet is that the firm focuses investment and vests its future in one particular outcome. This is the complete opposite of spreading investments among several possible scenarios, thereby maintaining flexibility to respond to an unknown outcome. In the big bet, flexibility is not a great virtue. Typically, you want to engage in this type of strategy when you believe you can strongly influence the outcome of the current uncertainty. Interestingly, while "shaping" strategy such as this is predominantly the purview of an extremely strong market player, it can also be leveraged by an extremely weak player as well. The idea is as follows. If you are a weak market player then you may recognize that if the uncertainty resolves a certain way you will not be able to compete. Your firm will go under. In this case, you may be better off making a big bet on a particular scenario where you can win big. The thinking would be: better to invest where there is risk and a payoff than where there is risk and loss of the investment.

Technically, as a pioneer making a big bet, you need not pour all your money into one particular project, though that is often the case. The big bet may be in one particular outcome or scenario. This could involve investing in multiple projects in order to produce the desired end-state. So, the investment need not be in new information technology, new product development, new manufacturing machinery or processes, and so forth. Indeed, using established products or technology to enter a new market may give you better survival odds than trying to develop new products in an already existing market.

The reason for this has to do in part with the concept of customer "stickiness" and education. If a market already exists, consumers will have established brand preferences. Those preferences can be overcome only with an education (read, expensive marketing or advertizing) campaign. If the item is relatively non-substitutable (like enterprise software), then that will be one very expensive, difficult, and risky educational campaign. By contrast, creating or entering a new market means consumers will likely not have established preferences. An educational campaign is still needed, but now it is about awareness, getting customers to try the product, not about getting them to change their preferences and behavior – a much harder feat to accomplish. One business study showed, for example, that firms entering the disk drive industry did better in new (e.g., music players), than old (e.g., PC), markets because as pioneers they avoided head to head competition with established players in the more mature markets.

Some Attributes of Pioneers

Pioneers have leveraged all sorts of attributes to establish early dominance. They have leveraged presence across different marketplaces, product line depth, pricing policies, R&D focus, capacity utilization, greater risk tolerance, and resource commitments that all reflected their unique strategic postures. Other, softer capabilities have been leveraged as well. Some pioneers, for example, have strong financial management skills and lower debt than their competitors. It is important to note that debt can affect entry timing; the greater your debt the later you will likely enter an emerging market.

By contrast, high costs are associated with entering markets early. These costs are not just in marketing (educating the consumer) but also in innovating. You might think, then, that the size of your R&D budget would influence market entry timing. Apparently not, even though pioneers generally speaking have been shown to incur greater R&D costs. Instead, a more important contributor to early market entry may be what is often referred to as "slack" – resources like finances or employees not essential to current operations that can rapidly be re-directed to new projects. Firms with slack have been shown to be more willing to experiment with innovating to enter new markets. Slack resources not only make operations more fluid, but they also reduce the risks associated with experimenting with new strategies, new products, and new markets. You can now absorb the costs associated with failure, because in a way you are already incurring them.

Firm size is not a particular determinant of who will be a pioneer. You can be large or small and engage in pioneer strategies. Perhaps it is the case that firms at both "tails" of the bell curve – the largest and the smallest firms – benefit most from pioneer strategies. Smaller firms certainly do so at the highest risk, however. Larger size implies increased market experience that can be translated by effective management into lowering barriers to entry (e.g., through alliances, brand leverage, etc.). In one study of the hard disk drive industry, market experience was correlated with earlier entry into new niches.

If experience does not necessarily equate with performance, how does performance affect the likelihood of being a pioneer? Viewed from this perspective, the data seems positively contradictory, including contradicting some of the observations just made above. One study suggested that the worse your overall market performance, the earlier you are likely to enter an emerging market – that pressure makes you start gambling a bit more. Other studies showed that the better you perform in your current market(s), the later you will enter any new ones. Microsoft certainly follows this model. Routinely it waits for others to prove market viability and penetration before it steps into the market itself. In some ways this makes sense. Better performing firms typically have the resources to wait and buy their way into a market (though this admittedly is making a size assumption). Lesser performing firms tend to cast about for a way to change the nature of the competition, specifically to escape it if it is too strong. They are thus more likely to be paying more attention to the environment looking for "escape hatches." A better performing firm by contrast is more likely to be seeking to invest in erecting barriers around its success rather than looking for alternative investment opportunities.

Do Pioneers Win?

Using databases to conduct statistical cross-firm studies and individual case studies, researchers have amassed an impressive amount of data to suggest pioneers do win in their competitive segments. This seems to hold true across both consumer and industrial goods sectors. By and large, the studies attempt to be consistent in differentiating between pioneers and early entrants, though they are not always successful. This lack of segregation produces some of the mixed results you will find in the discussion that follows. By this point you should be asking yourself just what the definition of success is that these studies use. In the chapter on advantage, success in the private sector was correlated with being profitable. Most of the studies on pioneers, however, focus on market share as the definition of success. This may be because market share is often assumed in the long run to equate to greater profitability. In the short run, that clearly is not the case. So you need to consider the issue of timeframe when undertaking a pioneer strategy. If the market cannot congeal and stabilize for the long term, being the pioneer will be a comparatively more expensive proposition.

So what does the research show? In the mature consumer goods sector, pioneers were found to have higher market shares than later entrants. On average, a pioneer could capture as much as 20% of the market.

An early entrant that rose to dominance could capture on average as much as 17% of the market. And a dominant later entrant could capture only 13% of the market on average, or roughly 65% of what an early entrant could capture. (Robinson and Fornell, 1985)

The same effect was found for mature industrial businesses, though the potential market shares were larger. Pioneers could achieve a market share of nearly 30%. A dominant early follower could achieve two thirds that in market share, or roughly 20%, and a dominant late follower could only manage to capture 15% of the same market. While the lower share for later entrants makes sense given that they likely faced more competitors dividing up the market, the research still indicates order of entry affected share. (Robinson, 1988).

Switching from mature to comparatively immature businesses, market share for early entrants is clearly higher. Late followers are constrained more than is the case in more mature markets. One study shows that, for startup businesses, market pioneers on average could achieve a market share of 24%. Compare that to less than half, or 10% market share, that a follower could expect to achieve on average. Among "adolescent" businesses, market shares were closer between first and later movers. Pioneers could amass over 30% of the market share. Early followers could expect to achieve a market share of roughly 20%. Interestingly, in this case late followers could achieve higher market shares – roughly 25% – suggesting that some particular attributes of the late followers allowed them to leap-frog the early followers. (Lambkin, 1988)

So what are some of the attributes that the studies pick up as affecting market share when tied to entry order? Unsurprisingly, they vary considerably, making it difficult to derive hard conclusions about what attributes firms should have before they embark on a pioneer strategy. In the mature industrials study, pioneers were shown to have higher product quality, broader product lines, and to serve markets more broadly. Another study on new corporate ventures in both consumer and industrial sectors concluded the same. Pioneers had higher quality products or offered better services, and they served the market more with greater selection than did later entrants. Finally, one study looked at spending and entry order, concluding that pioneers incurred greater marketing and R&D expenses than did followers. The implication of followers spending less than pioneers is important. Because the followers did not have to spend as much on R&D, and could leverage the pioneer's marketing expenditures, they were more profitable even with lower market share.

Turning from the database studies to the individual and survey-based business case studies, pioneer advantages can be seen again – though the results are more mixed. Where the case studies are usually limited is in the scope of what they assessed. In almost all cases, first movement is correlated with new product introduction. Sometimes the new product is for a new market, but the studies do not tease this aspect apart, leaving us to guess as to how the payoff differs between new product / old market versus new product / new market. The case studies do not address the old product / new market pairing discussed earlier in this chapter.

Clearly, research shows a pioneer benefit. In the pharmaceutical industry, one study of two categories of prescriptions drugs concluded that the first firm to offer and promote a new type of product received a substantial and enduring sales advantage. Later entrants could overtake the pioneer only by offering new benefits (such as reducing side effects). The same held true in a study of the cigarette industry. Studies of the semi-conductor industry show more mixed conclusions. One concluded that the first manufacturer to produce a design went on to reap the biggest market share (for that design). Another concluded that there was a negative correlation between entering first and holding market share. In the first case, the result was explained in part by the lengthy period required to qualify vendors, a form of distribution chain lead time. In the second, no attribute was found to explain the negative correlation, though quality and engineering skill were found to mitigate the negative effect.

Attributes other than internal capabilities accounted for some pioneer successes as well. A study of the medical diagnostic imaging market found that pioneer success were more correlated with a firm being new to market instead of established. Incumbents were found to perform better as followers than as pioneers, though no particular reason was provided why. Firms under profit pressure were also found to be better off as pioneers, although again cause and effect are not clear. Eastman Kodak's pioneering of the camcorder market is cited as a case in point. Kodak introduced the first camcorders in 1984, and the study attributed this pioneering move to profit traumas in the preceding two years caused by growing competition from Fuji Film.

The study also cited other pioneers like Amana (microwave oven), Hamilton (digital watch), and Magnavox (video games), which all reported a low return on sales prior to introducing their respective new products. In the household microwave oven market, Raytheon/Amana's Radarange microwave was the pioneer in the early 1960's. The market was fragmented because sales took off slowly. Litton's microwave oven, also introduced in the mid-1960's, was considered a pioneer as well. "Early" followers entered the market nearly a decade later when both Sharp and Sanyo introduced their models in 1973. A few years later Sunbeam (1977) and Samsung-Lucky Goldstar (1980's) became late followers with their models. Amana and Litton, both pioneers, wound up splitting the market.

Not to belabor a point, but don't confuse pioneers as always the literal first. Rather, you should focus on the pioneer who stays in the market and generates competition that sustains the market. There is obviously a cautionary tale here. You can be the first and die. But, paradoxical as it sounds, there can be more than one pioneer. Take for example, the low calorie beer market. There were three pioneers because the first two failed completely. Rheingold introduced Gablinger's in the 1960's followed by Meister Brau and its Lite brand, neither of which succeeded. Miller Lite was the first beer to sustain the market, so even though it was introduced into the market in 1975, it still was the pioneer. The earliest follower was Schlitz Lite in 1976, followed by Anheiser-Busch Natural Light in 1977, and Michelob Lite in 1978. Bud Light could be considered the late follower in 1981.

In the disposable diaper market, three pioneers emerged. First was Procter and Gamble's Pampers, introduced initially in 1961. That particular product introduction failed. Borden became the next pioneer with White Lamb in 1965 and Scott soon thereafter with Baby Scott's in 1966. That same year P&G re-introduced Pampers to the marketplace. The early followers were KC's Kimbles, Curity, and Scott again with a new brand, Raggedy Ann and Andy, all in 1971. The late followers were P&G again with Luvs in 1976, Scott again with Tots the same year, KC again with Huggies in 1977 and Johnson and Johnson in 1978. As of the study date, Pampers continued to dominate the market but showed signs of losing share to Huggies and its own Luvs. In this case, P&G could tolerate the cannibalization of market share from its own Pampers because the market was showing signs of moving toward wealth-influenced purchasing where its Luvs (and rival Huggies) enjoyed preeminence.

In the market for personal stereos, Sony was the clear pioneer when it introduced the Walkman in 1979. From 1980 through 1981 early followers Panasonic and Toshiba followed with their own versions. Sanyo and Aiwa were considered late followers when they came to market in 1982. In the pre-MP3 player period of this study, pioneer Sony continued to hold some 50% of the market.

Another market where Sony dominated was the VCR market. CBS teamed with Motorola to produce the first VCRs in the 1968-71 time period. Their product lost traction and AVCO tried to create the market anew with its Cartridge TV in 1972. Consumers still were not interested until the introduction of Sony's Betamax in 1975. Zenith and Sanyo entered the market at the same time, making all three pioneers in a still new market. Almost all other competitors entered simultaneously in 1977: Matsushita, Panasonic, Quasar, JVC, RCA, GE, Magnavox, Sylvania, and Sharp. Sony gained dominant market share on the basis of an extensive advertising campaign, but over time began losing share to the superior design of Matsushita – one of the followers.

How Pioneers Win

Successful pioneers tend to leverage a number of key advantages. Some pioneers reply upon their ability to invent new products in order to move first. Nike did this in the sneaker industry. Sony did it with the Walkman. Amana and Litton did it with microwaves, and GE practically invented the middle class home security market with its mass-produced Home Sentry product.

Other pioneers use their large advertising budgets and market clout to introduce new products and dominate new segments. Miller Lite used its market position to get bars to put its Lite beer on tap, which made it less expensive than bottled beer and more likely to be tried. Similarly, Procter and Gamble (Pampers) and Sony used their market clout to dominate distribution channels (the most common way of leveraging clout in the value chain) and to ease the co-branding process with consumers.

Still other pioneers leverage their ability to become the low cost producer to enter new markets and sub-markets. Texas Instruments (TI) is a case in point. TI figured out how to produce solid-state transistor calculators for less than anyone else in the market. They took what was an expensive piece of scientific equipment costing over $100 dollars and reduced it first to under $30 dollars and then even less than that. They then introduced the calculator into department stores for a new market constituency – students – leading to market dominance of hand-held calculators that lasted well over a decade. Even today TI still captures a significant share of the market that remains.

Overall, pioneers typically win because they achieve advantages that can be classified into five categories. The first of the five categories is economic: you gain concrete financial benefits over your competitors by moving first. The second is pre-emptive: you gain access to resources or markets that make it harder for follow-on competitors to obtain as well. The third is organizational / technological: you obtain the lead on technologies and organizations that work, and externally can begin to force competitors to compete on your terms. The fourth is customer behavior: you can create customer stickiness and otherwise influence customer behavior more so than can followers. The last category is political / legal: you develop the (legal) ability to secure more favorable treatment from the courts and political classes than can your later competitors. You should consider using these five categories as a framework for selecting the metrics by which you will measure the success of your strategy.

Looking at the economic category in more detail, you can gain advantages as a pioneer a number of ways. One is scale effect. Pioneers have the natural lead in ramping up to meet consumer demand. (If demand explodes, then early followers gain as well where pioneers cannot meet demand.) With size you can pool purchases, such as media buys, so that you pay less per unit than follow-on entrants who may be smaller. Even without size, you can acquire inputs (like plant equipment) and supplies at prices lower than what will prevail later when followers compete and bid up prices. In fact, you can achieve an absolute cost advantage over followers, not just a relative one. This pricing power apparently works in your favor the other way too. Data show that pioneers are able to establish product pricing that sticks. So while the number of competitors required to erode market share is low enough to beware of, the number of competitors required to erode pricing advantages is high. This suggests that pricing and thus profitability may be more sustainable than market share!

Pioneers also get to erect barriers to entry that help lock in profitability. Smarter firms do not focus exclusively on barriers to entry, as too many venture capital firms did during the 1990's internet boom. Barriers to entry work only between incumbents and newly entering competitors. In an entirely new industry, you may not even know who your competitors are. Consequently, you should focus instead on creating resource barriers. For example, leveraging technology to consolidate and scale back-office activities is an example of creating a resource barrier. This way even if the market or product entry barrier is low, the resource barriers may be high enough to prevent your competition from achieving significant market share or profitability.

In the second of the five categories, pre-emption, pioneers gain advantage by erecting competitive barriers apart from the obvious legal ones like patents. One example is occupying choice real estate. Retailers understand this better than anyone. But even manufacturers can locate where there are advantageous local tax incentives and then negotiate to bar the door to competitor entrants. Another example is pre-empting a range of scarce resources from upstream inputs (raw materials) to downstream channels (retailer shelf space). The same pre-emption can be done with human capital. Hiring the best of the crop (even beyond your current requirements) can remove talent needed by your competitors. Naturally, your competitors can respond by hiring from elsewhere geographically, poach talent from you (why non-competes are important), or train new hires extensively. All these responses, though, only serve to drive up your competitor's costs, yielding a cost advantage to you as the pioneer.

On the flip side, you need to be aware that the internet mitigates some of these benefits, to the point of being destructive to old business models. You cannot build scale in phone ordering systems if customers can go click online by themselves. You will have more difficulty locking in retailers if retailers are not needed for online shops (they may be a welcome adjunct, a 'clicks and bricks' strategy, but they are not a necessity for some products). So, before you go embarking on a strategy of pre-emption, make sure to test your strategy against potential internet rivals (or scenarios if you have sharp talent on your strategy team).

If what you offer, however, is technically complex, or requires complementary products and spare parts, then pre-emption can work. Large equipment manufacturers for pharmaceutical companies fit this category. Downstream channel partners may be reluctant to carry second and third brands because of the inventory requirements (e.g., parts) associated with selling large equipment. Pre-emptive dominance need not be entirely physical however. It can be psychological as well. Large pharmaceutical firms are able to create dominant awareness among prescribing doctors (ever notice all the branded doodads in your doctor's office?) such that they are achieving pre-emption by blocking the doctors from thinking about prescribing competitor products.

Even in the food industry channel blocking can occur. Take the case of Frito Lay, the chip company. Seeking to leverage its chip business into other products, Frito Lay succeeded in inventing shelf-stable chip dip with multiple flavors (confession: I love their bean dip, bad for you though it is). Having pioneered the product, Frito Lay now dominates because it got grocers to minimize the shelf space available to later entrants. This is why if you go to the grocery store, you will see other brand salsas on shelves under the chips, or down the aisle from the chips while Frito Lay's dips are on eye-level racks right in front of the chips. In some supermarkets, you literally have to reach past a can of dip to pick a bag of chips (not necessarily Frito Lay's, either) off the shelf.

In the third of the five categories, organizational / technological, pioneers can gain advantage a number of ways. On both technology and organization (including process capabilities) you can exploit your early learning and experience to reduce costs, such as through inventory control and inventing new manufacturing techniques. Organizationally, you can figure out how best to structure your firm's operations to manufacture products. You can experiment (and may want to if you are pioneering an entirely new market) and from that develop product and process innovations that you can embed into the firm so that they are less likely to be visible to competitors. The less visible the innovations are, the more they can be made inimitable. This then gives you solid market advantage. Meanwhile, you can turn your attention to learning which communications channels and messages work best for your target customer. In so doing, you can organize partnerships with external media outlets in ways that force followers to take more time to figure out.

On the technological side, you can achieve advantage greater than simply outpacing the market in technological upgrades. You get to figure out where processing bottlenecks are and then how to work around them in the scaling process. If the bottleneck is external, then you may even invent proprietary ways of helping your channel sellers, locking in parts of the distribution chain. The same can be said for upstream suppliers as well. And if you can dominate the supply chain both up and downstream then you may create a category standard that defeats entry by followers. This very model helps explain Avon's dominance of overseas sales over similar competitors.

In the fourth of the five categories, customer behavioral, pioneers gain advantage because of the control they wield over consumer stickiness, including how customers learn about their brand, product attributes, and so forth. Never lose sight of the fact that customers learn, whether intentionally or not. Your very presence in the market can influence customer learning even without advertising. You can define ideal attribute combinations, the importance of one product attribute over another, and otherwise influence consumer preferences. Starbucks has become a master at this. How many times have you heard someone order a coffee elsewhere and accidentally ask for a tall one rather than a small one? Add marketing to the mix, and you can create a perceptual structure of the market that works to your advantage. You may even be able to establish your product as the industry standard, or at least that is the goal. Then you can move onto version 1.1 when imitators are just getting their version 1.0 to market. Think Apple and the iPhone and iPad, and you get the idea.

In addition to the learning experience, the behavioral approach focuses also on the concept of the switching cost, which you can use to your advantage. A switching cost is when the customer incurs some type of cost giving up one product in favor of another. Enterprise level software is a classic example of a product with high-switching costs. The costs are not only attributable to the new purchase, but to ancillary needs as well, such as employee training, new hardware requirements, and so forth. These costs can be contractual as well, such as those "imposed" by long-term supplier agreements. By contrast, soap and cereal could be considered at the opposite end in terms of switching costs. The economic costs of switching are nil. But the psychological costs may be high. Customers have to search for alternatives and then decide which one to use. My wife tells a funny (but poignant) story that illustrates the point. In the early 1990's, right after the collapse of the Soviet Union, she ran into a couple of older Russian women in the cereal aisle of the local grocery. Recent arrivals to the U.S., they were positively paralyzed by the options they faced, even after my wife patiently explained it all to them. They just wanted to know what cereal they were "supposed" to buy.

Learning to use a new product also imposes its own form of psychological switching costs. Many customers simply do not want to have to learn how to use products (remember all those VCR's with blinking clocks stuck at 12:00). Many customers also do not want to incur the expense of searching for alternatives. They are likely to know more about the pioneer's offerings, and have more experience using them, than the followers' alternatives, and are comfortable with the information asymmetry that results. Customers will take on the burden of searching for alternatives only when the anticipated gain is greater than the cost of the search and switch.

When are switching costs likely the greatest? The behavioral advantage to the pioneer appears to be greater in the consumer than the industrial markets. In part this seems to occur because consumers rarely have an economic incentive to switch owing to minimal cost differences. After all, how much difference in price is there between bars of soap (generally speaking, of course)? Thus, brand awareness is likely to play a leading role in developing psychological switching costs. The economic advantage to the pioneer appears to be greater then the customer purchases with moderate frequency compared to fewer or greater purchase frequencies. Why moderate purchases? Well, they tend to be bigger ticket items like equipment, small enough not to require re-evaluation every time new ones are bought, but large enough to incur associated costs like learning. Also, with these types of purchases, say copiers for business, once the first one is bought the buyer is likely to seek cost reductions on further purchases and the seller is likely to want to lock in the customer, so both are incented to contractually obligate to each other.

In the last of the five categories, legal / political, pioneers gain advantage by leveraging their access to political leaders and aggressively seeking application of the law and regulations in their favor. The most obvious is protection under patent and other intellectual property laws. But advantage usually extends beyond these protections. For example, you may be able to get the government to protect a new "industry" with tariffs or duties. You may be able to establish benchmarks of price "controls" whereby you can shut out foreign competitors with anti-dumping or countervailing duties. As a pioneer, you may be able to influence trade agreements to your advantage. You may even be able to get the government to step in and privatize / re-privatize assets before competitors are able to enter the market. Anyone following Russian President Putin's activity in that country's oil industry has seen how governments can wreak havoc on the emergence of competitors.

Meanwhile, in emerging markets, pioneers can establish and then leverage favorable government relations to create a variety of obstacles to followers. Where governments control access to resources, perhaps through ownership or control of distribution channels (e.g., state railroad, state ports) you may be able to create bottlenecks to competition, so long as your state partners do not begin to act opportunistically, as Chinese partners tend to do. You may be able to get the government to restrict the number of licenses or permits that can be obtained (and then buy those up) as well. At a more sophisticated level you can work with legislatures or governing bureaucracies to influence the direction of regulatory change and compliance, keeping your competitors off-balance.

Leaving aside the "political connectedness" advantages associated with moving first in emerging markets, there are natural economic advantages to be obtained as well. First and foremost, pioneers – like Mary Kay cosmetics in China – may tap pent-up demand for "Western" brands that were previously unobtainable. This is true even for a smaller newcomer that leapfrogs over a hesitant larger player. Mary Kay sales representatives in China for a long time could point to the absence of Avon, the better-known brand, as the reason to buy their products.

Pioneer advantages in emerging markets can be subtle as well. If your brand is already known, you can lower marketing costs because you do not have to promote brand awareness or educate consumers. Or, you can lock in lower advertising rates. Within five years of the end of communism in Eastern Europe advertising rates had increased an order of magnitude, costing followers more to enter a market and promote brand awareness than it had cost the pioneers. Meanwhile, emerging markets also typically lack the infrastructure to support more than a few advertising channels – maybe a few newspapers, a couple of radio stations, and the like. This means you can dominate the few channels that exist, and potentially even lock up favored treatment through contracts. Finally, you can develop a pool of experienced marketing managers that allow you to stay ahead of competition trying to enter the same market.

How Pioneers Lose

The reasons why pioneers may lose do not necessarily mirror those that led to success. This is why it is important to touch on this topic, even if only briefly. It is not enough to avoid doing the opposite of what it takes to win. That said, since much of this discussion dovetails with reasons why pouncers win, and that is the subject of the next chapter, consider the following discussion a brief preview.

To start with, shifting customer preferences play a role in the failure of pioneers. This occurs when you are not able to establish the dominant design and are unaware you have not done so. Thus, you can enter markets first, acquire competitive capabilities, and still fail in the competitive environment because the dominant design emerges later. Initially, you may survive because the lack of design standardization allows followers to occupy niche segments. But if the dominant design turns out to emerge from one of these niche segments, then you can fail. Take the example of MP3 (portable music) players. Apple was a later entrant to the market; yet the hip, sleek design of its iPod (and iconic commercials) has made it the dominant product. This uncertainty over ultimate design preferences creates its own dynamic around market entry timing about which you have to be constantly vigilant.

Even patents are no guarantee of pioneer protection. One study shows that within four years of a patent, successful innovations are imitated roughly two thirds of the time. Later entrants simply invent "around" the patent by changing key elements to make the product different enough to merit a new patent. Take an example I consulted on in the bakery sector. A food "printer" was invented to "spray" color dye pictures on baked goods like cake icing. The idea was that the baked item could be placed on a tray and a plotter-like printer would spray a scanned-in picture onto the icing. A patent was taken out on the printer and printing process. What did I find a competitor doing? Well, they created a smaller printer that sprayed the dye onto edible rice paper, which was then placed on top of the icing. The competitor invested, smaller, cheaper equipment that was easier to use, and ultimately beat out the first patented approach. The lesson to keep in mind is that if you are a pioneer relying on patent protection, you put yourself at some risk. You have to avoid becoming complacent and developing a false sense of market advantage. This is particularly true in most technology-related areas, which is susceptible to reverse engineering. Patents can be "worked around," sometimes more easily than you might suspect.

In a related vein, pioneers in rapidly developing industries are at risk as well. By the time legal barriers work in their favor, the industry may have moved on to new designs and/or processes. Rapid or discontinuous market shifts can give followers the ability to take advantage of newer or larger numbers of gateways to the market. For example, Palm's attempts to put phones on its personal digital assistant (PDA) devices failed at the same time as cell phone makers figured out how to put calendaring and contact software on their phones. As Palm and its clone Handspring discovered, major shifts in technology caught them ill-prepared because their investment in hardware trapped them, while cell phone makers like Samsung, were not burdened with the same investment. The latter could leverage their existing product platform but change the software – a very different cost proposition from Palm's need to create new hardware. Nearly all learning associated with being the pioneer became irrelevant, and Palm has since become an insignificant player in the market.

Yet another danger to pioneers comes from time-related traps of a kind different from those discussed earlier. There is the threat of becoming addicted to change – of constantly re-inventing the company because change is embraced for change's sake, rather than because the customer base wants it. A related problem is confusing time-based competition with simply moving fast. Time-based competition still must adhere to the customers' decision and preference time-cycles. Competition based on simple speed- risks outstripping the customers' time-cycles, leading to negative consequences. Many Japanese firms discovered in the 1980's that by competing on speed, they accidentally disconnected their marketing from their operational time-cycles, and then from their customers' cycles. At first, speeding up worked. Firms began responding faster to shifts in consumer tastes. Over time, however, those firms began to front-run consumer tastes, guessing at what consumers wanted at greater and greater scale levels. This then required larger and more expensive marketing efforts to get the consumer to want something new. Firms were incurring greater costs re-educating consumers rather than scaling up to meet current tastes. You can see the result at the annual Las Vegas Consumer Electronics Show today where thousands of companies tout all kinds of digital products for which there is little to no established consumer demand. Indeed, those shows have become a centerpiece for companies trying to kick-start consumer demand – otherwise they are dead.

A Final Thought

It would seem, based on the discussion thus far, that pioneers gain dominance when they establish the dominant design at the outset or are able to respond competitively enough to the emergence of a later, different design. That is, the pioneer must have the ability to change its own product technology to avoid obsolescence in case its design turns out not to be the dominant one. The evidence to date does not suggest that pioneers – not to mention most firms overall – are capable of this kind of radical change.

Indeed, there seems to be an implicit big bet taken by most pioneers that is difficult to overcome. One study found that an astounding half of them failed rapidly. They were able to maintain their front-runner position for only five years. By contrast, early market followers (not pioneers) failed at a fraction of the leader rate – roughly only a tenth. Such numbers suggest that disadvantages of being a pioneer are daunting indeed. It is difficult enough being right, let alone being right first. Essentially, though, this is what is required of the pioneer in order to be successful. That characteristic is what makes this strategy the highest risk one of the three presented here.

4 POUNCER STRATEGY

The goal of pouncer strategy is to develop an advantage or advantages that allows you to follow the pioneers rapidly into the market with a more desirable offering so that you surpass and dominate over the pioneer. Unlike pioneers who move first, when gains are unclear, pouncers position themselves to be able to rapidly follow the pioneer once the gains are clear. Pouncers wait because they prefer achieving dominance over mere follower status, and believe that they have the strength to unseat pioneers.

Note a key difference between pouncers and late followers – competitors who enter after pouncers. Late followers wait essentially until market uncertainty is resolved, and therefore need no strategy for uncertainty. Theirs is the luxury of leveraging any one of a number of normal business strategies for mature (or maturing) markets. As a result, however, late followers generally do not come to dominate the market they enter. They are usually relegated to being either niche players or just simply smaller competitors. Pouncers by contrast are usually seeking to dominate over the pioneer(s), and therefore need to move sooner to wrest the dominant market share their way.

If late followers bear almost no risk of determining market direction, pouncers do bear some risk of guessing wrong on market direction. Typically marketing and sales powerhouses, they carefully watch the competition trying to define market direction, then enter. Still, they can be wrong because they are generally entering an immature market. There are other risks as well. The chief one is of waiting too long to pounce. Like a surfer, pouncers really do have to catch the right wave at the right time. Fail to do that and they risk getting into the market too late, being left behind, and ultimately being a non-threat who gets run out of business by bigger competitors (particularly when scale is a key competitive advantage).

Two core strategies can be leveraged to become a pouncer. One is time-pacing (ironically, in much the same vein as pioneers). The other strategy is building the ability to imitate swiftly the right moves your competitors make in the market. The ability to imitate can itself be further deconstructed. One possibility is to develop the ability to market better than competitors can. The other is to build flexible processes and/or flexible organizational structures that can adjust rapidly to the emerging market.

Success as a pouncer lies in understanding that achieving imitability is the key driver of your actions during the period of uncertainty! That is, you have to position yourself to be able to imitate whatever product or service emerges as the dominant market winner, as it is emerging. As so many start-up firms (and their venture backers) discovered during the dot com bubble, achieving imitability is not so easy even when throwing other people's money at it.

A labyrinth of obstacles explains why start-ups failed to imitate the pioneers. First, there is the problem of what some call "causal ambiguity," or the inability to understand why something is working in the market. The pioneer may have hidden advantages or capabilities (like intellectual property or human experts) that are critical to success, but largely unseen to the outside observer. Or, there may be a certain complexity to the way processes are run, or how software interacts, that mask what is really going on. Then, there is the obstacle of what you might call time compression. Simply put, the attempt to catch up to the pioneer can be very difficult to accelerate. Never mind simply trying to catch up. If for some reason you cannot unseat the pioneer in the marketplace then you have to get past them even as they are still moving forward. Acceleration is thus required, and achieving it in a new market, or with a new technology, or with a new organizational structure, is no easy task. Meanwhile, bureaucratic obstacles work against acceleration. Regulatory review periods are an example. If building permits are required, that can eat up valuable time necessitating even greater acceleration later. Another obstacle working against acceleration is called value chain dominance, and you see it when pioneers tie up scarce resources, say, by owning scarce mineral mines, or contracting to tie up all viable suppliers, etc.

Overcoming these obstacles cannot occur in a vacuum. The mistake you risk making is assuming that the pioneer will not survive competition. This is simply not true. Being the pouncer does not automatically make you the heir apparent. The pioneer ultimately may fail, but not before killing you. Just as pioneers can die in the market (like last chapter's discussion of lite beers), so can you as the pouncer. Ultimately, "third" or "fourth" movers may emerge as the winners. So, even as you strive to achieve imitability, you do so under the scrutiny of rivals. This means that you not only have to achieve imitability in the technical sense of being able to execute in the emerging market (i.e., make the product, organize correctly, whatever), you still have to do so while protecting yourself from later entrants.

By this point, the emphasis on acceleration should clue you in that time-based strategy can be more important than capabilities-based strategy as a pouncer. Indeed, as you may recall from the Chapter One discussion, fans of hyper-competition view time as an explicit competitive driver. Very much an internet-age argument, hyper-competition was an implicit philosophy of venture firms seeking to fund all sorts of pouncer firms going online, but was conveniently forgotten when it came to thinking about how those firms would survive with all the follow-on competitors. Nevertheless, it does have an important role to play in pouncer strategy.

So what are some of the ways to leverage time to pick up speed on the pioneer? Well, you can (and should) take advantage of how rapidly technology diffuses into the marketplace to drive competition against pioneers. For example, the migration online of what were once internally-based technologies has given rise to whole new online infrastructure and back office capabilities that did not exist just a few short years ago. Leveraging these new, online capabilities can open up access to resources that the pioneer thought they had locked up, particularly in overseas markets.

Alternatively, you can reduce investment or time to market by outsourcing non-critical activities. You can thus leverage a smaller staff to get more done operationally. Simultaneously, you can gain increased speed to make tactical adjustments responding to the market. In the PC segment, for example, pouncers outsource component manufacturing to focus on overall product design. The pouncer thus lets others do what they do best while focusing on what it does best to unseat the pioneer.

Another tactic is to collaborate with the pioneer to try to evolve a new industry standard that allows you to compete faster (by adding drag to the unwitting pioneer trying to adjust to the new standard). Conversely, you can seek to codify the current standard when you believe you can lock in the pioneer's ability to innovate, but that you can move faster to woo and overtake the customer base.

Some Attributes of Pouncers

What attributes of a firm make it a pouncer likely to win in the marketplace? Size certainly has a correlation, and in this case it leans towards smaller entrant (though that need not always be the case). This is because large firms have sunk costs that, no matter how much economists say shouldn't happen, influence decisions about future investments. Sunk costs create the perception of higher exit costs that make larger firms more cautious in their entry decision.

Another correlate of pouncers is that they exhibit strengths across multiple capabilities. They tend to possess complementary assets that allow them to outperform the pioneer by having some combination of strong financials, branding, product experience, marketing services (especially market intelligence), competitive manufacturing capabilities, after-sale support, etc. In the PC industry, IBM was a case in point. With its significant computer expertise, strong financials and reputation, Big Blue entered the PC market late and still defeated the early entrants such as Apple and Tandy. Usually, successful pouncers typically demonstrate strong management experience and ancillary capabilities relevant to the market they enter. Tiny Netflix did this by combining mail-order distribution management at the national level with ease of online ordering and a very novel pricing strategy to force the large video chains (Blockbuster and Hollywood Video) into bankruptcy. Being able to manage operations across product and geographic lines also correlates speed of market entry. Note that "new" here has a relative meaning. Smart pouncers do not seek to enter markets where they have to learn too many new things. Instead, they usually enter where they can leverage previously learning and seemingly relevant standard operating procedures.

A key strategic success factor for pouncers is that they tend to focus on differentiating their product or themselves from the pioneer, one of the two competitive strategies favored by Wharton professor and strategist Michael Porter. Pouncers do so through superior market positioning. Perrier, for example, tapped nascent health consciousness of the early 1980's, beat out soda water rivals by affecting a snooty French and all-natural product attitude. IBM positioned its PC as a non-secretarial, broader business tool, in part by donating vast numbers of them to educational institutions where they could be used for social and natural science research in place of card readers attached to mainframes. It is interesting to note what these companies did not do. Traditional consumer models show that late comers to a market with an already established dominant brand often incur ruinous price competition. Successful pouncers, generally speaking, do not fall into this trap, as these companies did not.

Instead, pouncers have one of two differentiation strategies they can pursue, weak or strong differentiation, each with different "flavors." In the weak differentiation strategy, the pouncer can be a head-to-head challenger. Google Android cell phones taking on Apple iPhone is a classic example. The differentiation strategy is based on user and brand preferences. Price remains essentially the same to consumers. Also in the weak differentiation category, a pouncer can establish itself as an alternative, but essentially me-too, product. Purex positioning itself as an alternative to Clorox is an example of this type of me-too strategy. This can of course be coupled with a low-cost element to attract customers, but should not be confused with being a low-cost clone product, which would be more in keeping with the second, low-cost strategy described by Michael Porter.

Taken far enough, me-too strategies can lead pouncers to improve on products to the point that they consolidate the market around their copy-cat product. In the video tape sector, Sony was the standard that opened the market but Matsushita was able to change market demand to the VCR format and make it more widely available. Big Blue, IBM, was not the first to market PC's; Commodore, Apple, and Tandy held that distinction (does anyone remember the TRS-80?). But by combining PC's with disk drives, an operating system, and encouraging development of word processing and spreadsheet software, IBM made PCs a productive tool rather than a novelty. Apple did not invent the MP3 player nor downloadable music, but by combining the iPod with the iTunes store, it created within months a music hardware and software juggernaut that has proved difficult to dethrone. Finally, Google did not invent the online search engine, but thus far has beat out Yahoo, Altavista, and a host of others with both better interface design and more user-relevant search results.

In a high differentiation strategy, a pouncer can be a direct challenger to the dominant product, but with a very clear distinction that consumers understand right away. An example here is when Honda entered the US motorcycle market. In order to compete against Harley Davidson, Honda offered motorcycles with smaller engines that required less gas and also cost less than the famous "Hogs." In this case, there was a high product design and a high price differentiation strategy pursued at the same time. Another example is Microsoft's office suite. Each of it's core applications competed against a similarly priced market standard – Word against WordPerfect, Excel against Lotus-123, and Powerpoint against Harvard Graphics. What Office offered at first was standardization between applications – information could be easily shared between Excel and Word, for example, in a way that Lotus could not do easily with WordPerfect. Later, as office gained market scale, that standardization effectively occurred between businesses, cementing its place in the market.

Alternatively, instead of positioning as a direct challenger, the pouncer can pursue what might be called a fringe strategy. A humorous, but successful, case here would be the creation of the car rental firm Rent-a-Wreck. Their cars might be the same, brand-wise, as what a renter would find at Hertz or Avis, but their condition certainly is not. As such, prices are just low enough to make sense for the consumer and still leave the seller with enough profits to keep their fleet running.

Which of these high- or low- differentiation strategies is most likely to succeed? Research suggests that either one is acceptable if coupled with high prices rather than low prices. This is apparently due to asymmetries in customer preferences. If the pioneer has influenced these preferences, pouncers will have difficulty moving customers if there is a low price difference. Charlie Munger, Warren Buffet's investing partner, once famously explained the point this way. Say you are in a third world country. You go to a market and there are two packs of gum you can buy. One is a local brand you've never heard of, and the other is Wrigley's. For the difference of a dime in price, are you going to take the chance that the local gum will be as good? That is the power of a brand. And one already established in a low-price category, like gum or soda, is very difficult to dislodge.

By contrast, differentiated entry into a high-priced market, coupled with a price difference significant enough to grab a customer's attention, has a higher likelihood of success. Differentiation here does not necessarily mean radically altering the basics of the dominant design. Rather, a better sub-strategy is to shift from competing on design to competing by adding value to the dominant design. This way the switching costs that pioneers attempt to impose on consumers are diminished. Apple's iPod again is a case in point. The basic design features of the portable digital music player had already been set. What Apple did was use its' design expertise to add a more hip interface to the same product; use their marketing expertise to reach a wider, less computer oriented audience; and finally, marry the product with a legally available, large music selection to make the product more usable. Several other studies confirm this tendency for a high-differentiation strategy to succeed when the differentiation focuses on quality over pure function. This holds true across all kinds of market segments, from technology to pharmaceuticals, like the anti-ulcer drug market.

While on this theme, innovation can be highly correlated with pouncer success, especially when it is closely tied to developing internal learning capabilities. The trick, of course, is not to take it so far as to bet the company. This means accepting that new ideas are necessary for building on existing expertise, rather than inventing new knowledge. This can be done, for example, through cross-pollination of ideas between innovators or company change agents and those with deep expertise. Accepting this principle starts at the top with leaders who are open to new ideas even when those values seem to challenge established practices and core capabilities. Failure to accept change at the top leads to the rest of the company adopting a defensive objective of taking home paychecks, at the long-term expense of shareholders.

Many firms are probably guilty of this mistake. Keds and Converse both failed to see the rise of running shoes, allowing Nike and Reebok to enter and surpass them in the athletic shoe market. Kendall allowed Pampers to take it over in the disposable diaper market. IBM killed Digital in the microcomputer market. Bowmar and others all got overtaken by Texas Instruments in the electronic calculator market. United Airlines missed the development of the air freight forwarding market despite being first to offer the service. Even Levi's managed to miss the designer jeans market.

Do Pouncers Win?

Research shows that pouncers certainly win across market segments, not just in limited areas like technology. For example, in the running shoes market the pouncer not only surpassed two pioneers, but it also successfully shut out or relegated to niche status the later entrants. The two pioneers in this case were Adidas and Puma, who branched out from other sports (tennis and basketball) to cater to the nascent interest in running for fitness. Nike moved into the market, rapidly displacing the two pioneers. Three other companies subsequently tried to enter the same market: Brooks, Etonic, and New Balance. Of the three, only New Balance survived, mostly because it developed a reputation for catering to the road race crowd (with the best cushioning, which Nike later adopted) and to those with hard to fit, wide feet (Nike's were particularly known to be narrow).

In the diet soft drink market, Coke and Pepsi were not the pioneers. That honor went to a series of other firms that tried and failed, mostly on their own, until Coke developed a category killer to knock out the last pioneer. The pioneers here were two companies, Cott and Kirsch, that both developed no-calorie sodas in the 1950s. They largely failed on their own, to be supplanted by the third pioneer – Royal Crown in the early 1960s. Royal Crown did not get much time to establish its presence in the market, though. Introducing Diet Rite in 1962, RC (as the company is still known) quickly faced competition the next year in the form of Coke's Tab. Tab quickly took market share even as Pepsi introduced its Patio that same year. When Patio flopped, Pepsi re-entered the market with Diet Pepsi in 1964. Both Coke and Pepsi pushed all other contenders to niche status, and prevented successful follow-on entrants by leveraging their large marketing budgets to develop brand recognition through massive advertising (that has continued to this day).

In the small household appliance sector, the smoke detector market was an extremely dynamic one in the 1970s. General Electric (GE) was the first entrant, coming to market in 1972. It then followed up with the Home Sentry in 1975. GE was followed in rapid succession by Pyrotronic and Emhart in 1975, and then Teledyne, Gillete, Norelco, and Pittway all in 1976. Being the behemoth, GE managed to hold on to the dominant position for several years. However, Pittway's First Alert began to take over market share, eventually supplanting GE. Today, First Alert is still one of, if not the, leading smoke detectors in the market.

In the technology sector, it's worth taking a quick look at both the PC and the electronic calculators segments. Apple and Tandy Corporation are often considered to be the first entrants in the personal computer market, having introduced their respective products at the same time in 1977. Actually, like the diet soda market there was an even earlier entrant that failed by moving too early — Altair in 1972. Only one pioneer survived to become a niche player (albeit a significant one) in the PC market – Apple. There were two later entrants, IBM and Osborne, and the outcome is well known by now. IBM quickly came to dominate the PC while beating back all other product configurations, in particular the Apple Mac. Significantly, IBM's success was so great that it spawned a host of imitators, called clones, who were able to expand the dominance of the IBM PC configuration. Ironically, they did so to the point of commoditizing the PC and slowly driving IBM itself out of the market.

The market for hand-held calculators was little different. Canon was the first entrant with a commercial calculator, introducing the Pocketronic in 1970. Bowmar quickly followed with the Bowmar Brain only a year later. The market in this case, as with PCs, went to the later pioneer – Texas Instruments, which introduced its TI series in 1972 at a price point that made it accessible to the casual consumer. Within less than a year TI moved into first place in the market and dominated it for nearly a decade. As with PCs, it inspired a rash of low-cost foreign imitators who helped expand the market by commoditizing what was once viewed as a luxury electronics good, slowly loosening it's grip on the marketplace. Then, Hewlett Packard entered the market, leveraging its competency in engineering to re-design both the hardware and software for hand-held calculators. The software re-design in particular appealed to hard core math users (from engineering to finance to academia). The result was a calculator that quickly rose to dominance – particularly at the college level – and is still is the industry standard for all business school graduates.

How Pouncers Win

At its core, you win as a pouncer when you learn something from the pioneer or from the market that allows you to surpass the pioneer. There are many ways of accomplishing this. In the crassest form of learning, you can reverse engineer the pioneer's product. That way you can reduce or eliminate research and development costs and time. You can then sell the same product for less. Stepping up a level, you can analyze and capitalize on pricing and other mistakes made by the pioneer. For example, you can slipstream behind the substantial pioneering costs incurred by the pioneer, such as the expense of gaining regulatory approvals, educating potential buyers, nurturing suppliers, and developing infrastructure facilities. You can then leverage those to enter the market more quickly or cheaply. This does not automatically mean that you price yours products lower. You may in fact be able to mimic the pioneer's pricing. Because you have not incurred all the up-front costs of the pioneer, however, you become more profitable to your shareholders.

Pouncers need not only take advantage of pioneer investment costs. If your firm is skilled in marketing influence and shaping customer preferences, you can gain a differentiation advantage even where you do not have a cost advantage. You can actively force costs onto pioneers as well, especially "switching costs." You may recall from the prior chapter that this was discussed as an advantage to the pioneer, that pioneers are able to hold on to customers because the latter has some level of investment in the pioneer's product that prevents them from easily switching to the pouncer's product.

So what's different here? Customers are not the only party with investments. The pioneer obviously has them as well. Therein lies the opportunity for you as the pouncer: to drive enough change in the market so that it exceeds the pioneers' ability to switch. To the extent that the pioneer's investments are irreversible, the pioneer is said to be "locked-in." It cannot adopt (or can at unprofitable cost) the tactics of the following entrant. Alternatively, should the pioneer then attempt to regain ground by extending its product line to the new market design, it may be viewed as hypocritical or at least inconsistent and begin to lose customers that way. Note that IBM did not make this mistake. Interestingly, the case can be made that Apple founder Steve Jobs did so after he was forced out of Apple and attempted to start the Next computer. Next was viewed as too much like a regular PC and thus Jobs was viewed as being untrue to his roots. Compound the error with the fact that the Next was more expensive than a regular PC, and success became a long shot.

Some markets are probably more susceptible to pouncer success. Markets with lengthy product life cycles, such as durable consumer goods, appear to be one example. Followers here have more time to observe and learn from both the pioneer and market dynamics. Hyper-competitive markets like e-commerce would seem not as likely to spawn pouncer success. That said, many early dot coms made the mistake of waiting to go to market until they had erected barriers to entry based on patents. Unfortunately, some of the patents were overtaken by other technology and processes by the time they were issued, and in other cases patent "squatters" still won the market and later paid far less in court costs for violating the patent than they made in profits.

Pouncers do not have to rely solely on learning from pioneers to defeat them. There is learning from and influencing the markets themselves. You may be able to identify and exploit an overlooked product niche for example. You can undercut the pioneer's process. You can out-advertise to win greater consumer mind share. You can out-distribute the pioneer and steal market share in outright head-to-head competition. You can even overtake the pioneer by developing a reputation for innovating faster than the pioneer. The irony in this situation can be delicious. A pioneer invents the market but you later gain the credit and reputation as being the innovative one, either in product or strategy. Gillette, for example, has gained a reputation as the innovative player in shaving because of its strategy of continuous product improvements (who knew that shaving with four blades and a ruffle is so much better than with a triple blade?). Apple's iPod has gained the reputation as the innovator by coming to market with newer, better, and stylized portable music players – even though it was some three to four years late to the market.

Taking a step back from the concrete to the more conceptual, as a pouncer you can also leverage time and flexibility as key ways to beat pioneers. With respect to time, you want to eliminate time inefficiencies throughout your defined "time to market" processes. Paradoxically, a key way you can do so is to build flexibility into your organizations, systems, or processes so that you can nimbly adapt to the emerging reality. I say paradoxically because, to eliminate time inefficiencies, you have to accept other inefficiencies.

Another key way that you can eliminate time is to focus on your manufacturing processes. Here, there are three dimensions of time-based manufacturing to consider. First, you can try to develop a shorter product development-to-sales time, incrementally introducing innovations by building one upon the other in shorter periods of time. The point is to avoid making radical and thus expensive changes often. Facebook and Google are two examples that spring immediately to mind. Second, you can try to re-arrange the organization of your business processes so that workflow moves smoothly and, perhaps more importantly, can be re-arranged to shorten the manufacturing time cycle when clarity emerges. Finally, you can try to reduce the complexity of scheduled processes if you can determine that simpler processes will yield you time execution benefits.

Through all of these time-oriented approaches, you can reduce the need for long lead planning times. This gives you the further luxury of being able to wait a bit longer for clarity to emerge in the marketplace before acting to enter. To execute on this, you may want to switch from an annual planning process (the norm at most firms) to a rolling (perhaps quarterly) process. Such planning becomes more focused on short-term innovations, like upgrades, rather than longer-term innovations, like radical design changes. The idea here is that you should strive to develop two capabilities. First, be able to operate on a more rapid time cycle so that you can go head-to-head with the pioneer as market uncertainty lifts. Second, be able to place yourself closer to the winning product design (whether by imitation or substitution) so that you incur lower costs making the transition to the dominant design than the pioneer may have made.

The point here is not to make the mistake of focusing only on time. You cannot forget the importance of flexibility. For example, you may actually wind up in the short run increasing the time it takes to manufacture a particular product or the time it takes to makes a sale (though as you come to market you will need to shorten them). What you lose in current time you should be able to make up for in the ability to develop the right product for the market that emerges. So, say you decide that the dominant software design might be a more expensive enterprise version than the one you sell today. You may decide to hire salespeople who can readily sell enterprise software, but who may have more difficulty and thus take longer selling your current software. In this example, you clearly incur a penalty in the short run in exchange for the flexibility to sell right away into the new market.

To wrap up, you should focus on developing two sets of advantages – time and flexibility – if a pouncer strategy is your preferred option. Of course, both advantages can be symbiotic. Time is certainly an advantage in and of itself. Flexibility, though, can create time advantages either in your current processes or, more likely, in terms of developing a future ability to accelerate as the uncertainty clears. And, in turn, flexibility can be an advantage in and of itself. Flexibility can give you the ability to enter an emerging market because you now have the ability to try variety (e.g., making or selling the new product) at a lower cost than would be the case for non-flexible companies. You might argue at this point that the pouncer is acting more like a portfolio strategist than merely a pouncer. That is true. There is a definite overlap in the two strategies – in the development of flexibility and the creation of options that the pouncer can leverage. But further discussion on that is for the next chapter.

How Do Pouncers Lose?

Superior market learning does not automatically translate to success. There are still a number of key organizational elements that must be in place for you to dominate pioneers. As discussed in the prior chapter, some human and organizational resources are difficult to imitate. But that can make them difficult to change as well, something you will have to pay attention to on a sector by sector basis. In the automotive market, for example, there was little market in the United States for fuel-efficient cars, that is, until the 1973-74 energy crisis. That crisis gave Japanese car firms the market opening they needed as demand for their smaller cars soared with gas prices. What provided ultimate success was not so much that they were ready for the market, but that their American counterparts could not imitate the basis of success. American car manufacturers at the end of the day were slow to respond to Japanese innovations, fundamentally because their human and organizational assets were not attuned to developing and producing fuel-efficient cars. Nor were they interested in doing so. Their marketing departments did not believe Americans wanted small cars, despite all the growing data to the contrary. Let this be a lesson. If you cannot (or will not) build a strong business intelligence / market analysis function, or will not listen to them, you have little chance of success as a pouncer.

Timing when to enter the market can be another obstacle. Enter too late and you will face steep entry barriers that pioneers have been able to raise, in the form of economies of scales, brand name, manufacturing experience, and so forth. Also, as a pouncer you inevitably start with lower market share, and that creates vulnerabilities to market stamina. Entering markets sooner can increase your odds of survival when the pioneer has not yet gained critical customer mass. On the other hand, enter too early and profits may be lost to later entrants. Here's the dilemma you face in a nutshell. The fast imitator who is more like a co-pioneer may not erode the pioneer's wealth greater than a set of pouncers who follow later.

One of the key competencies of a pouncer, that of flexibility, can be your undoing as well. The more obvious point here is that in trying to maintain flexibility you may spread your resources so thinly that you will lose regardless of market positioning. The slightly less obvious point is that pioneers, by being more established, may develop routines and resources that enable them to deal with change more systematically. Start-up pouncers (as opposed to pouncers that are more established) have their own particular set of problems here. The lack of standardized routines can make them less able to adapt to technological design competition because they can get locked in to the existing design. Alternatively, they may not have the discipline (developed from standardized routines) to move through several designs one after the other. Because of this, start-up pouncers are highly susceptible to being drummed out of a market.

That last point highlights other firm-threatening problems. This may seem obvious, but bears repeating; you risk not developing expertise in any one thing when you try to do too much simultaneously. Parallel processes place increased financial and management strains on the company. Some level of inefficiency is inherent in the pouncer strategy. Care has to be taken, however, that it doesn't grow to the point of threatening your firm. When that happens, clearly flexibility has run amok. What happens next is that the leadership team needs to be removed, the number of products pared back, and perhaps even whole segments of the company replaced. During this time, the pouncer can suffer its final indignity: it gets locked out of the market because of an ill-timed yet thoroughly necessary reorganization.

A Final Thought

If the scenario above encapsulates the highest risk of the pouncer strategy, that does not make it the highest risk strategy overall. This is because you can await the resolution of uncertainty longer than the pioneer can. You also get to learn from the mistakes of the pioneer, even if in the process you risk getting locked out of certain resources or key customer bases. Finally, by focusing on improving internal processes so that you can move faster than the pioneer, you may paradoxically open up the opportunity to move first should you find that circumstances warrant doing so. You can plan to be a pouncer, and in the process pre-empt even yourself. The trick is realizing you are no longer a pouncer and switching to a pioneer strategy and following it (creating customer stickiness, pre-empting resources, developing scale, and so forth).

This particular paradox makes pursuing a pouncer strategy theoretically a lower risk one than a pioneer strategy. Practically speaking, it may not be lower risk if you cannot make the switch effectively to a pioneer strategy or can't build the advantages fast enough. This is why the pouncer strategy is still not the lowest risk strategy that can be pursued. That distinction will become evident in the next chapter.

5 HEDGING STRATEGY

No single firm should expect it can be a successful pioneer or pouncer all the time. Pioneers at some point in time will be compelled to move later. Pouncers inadvertently may be compelled into being a pioneer, or may be too late to market. Because of this, you may want to consider a strategy for achieving sustainable competitive advantage beyond that conferred by entry order. There is an alternative strategy set that can position you to win both by shaping or reacting correctly to the resolution of uncertainty, but with lower risk than is created by the pioneer and pouncer strategies. The alternative that maximizes the opportunity to win while minimizing the risk of missing the right market move is the hedging strategy.

In the context of market uncertainty, the goal of the hedging strategy is to develop one or more competitive advantages that are not part of your current set of competencies. At its most benign, a hedge-developed advantage may seem merely out of place among your existing competencies. More likely however, the new advantage runs counter to one or more of your current competencies. So why do it? Why make the investment? You do it so that as the uncertainty resolves you do not find yourself in a completely failed position.

Hedging strategy helps avoid the large forecasting errors typical of pioneer and pouncer strategies. Hedgers may move first or second or even later. Indeed, market entry order is secondary to the primary strategy of developing alternatives during the period of uncertainty. Like pouncers, but unlike pioneers, hedgers lower the risk of guessing wrong on both the market resolution or their ability to influence that resolution. Unlike pouncers, hedgers lower the risk of developing the wrong sets of capabilities to move rapidly.

So what does hedging strategy mean in the market context? It means building one or more abilities (resource, asset, capability, or competency) that runs counter to the firm's existing abilities. Put another way, hedging entails simultaneously investing in one or more abilities that compete with the firm's ongoing business. For example, a saddle maker who develops the ability to stitch car seats is hedging the demise of horses as a main mode of transportation. An investor may invest in two competing companies, hedging against the failure of one. In this case, the investor is deliberately placing a negatively correlated bet in which the overall portfolio still grows even if only one option emerges as the "winner." A hedge can be made with one investment. It can also be made with many. Be careful here. Buying into many different capabilities should raise the question of whether they are truly countering each other. When investing in multiple hedges, they should not only hedge against failure of the firm's current path, they should also hedge against each other as well.

When investments are made in multiple hedges, the firm is said to be creating a portfolio of hedges. Buying a portfolio of direct hedges in the form of outright abilities can get very expensive – too much so for small and medium-sized firms. This is where the concept of options becomes important. Instead of buying hedges outright, firms can buy "options" that in turn provide the capacity to buy the hedge outright at a later point in time. Financial markets understand this concept the best. Instead of buying a portfolio of stocks that balance each other, investors can (on a short-term basis) buy a basket of options underlying each stock for far less than the basket of stocks themselves. They can then "exercise" one or more options when it makes profitable sense to do so, but before the option expires.

This use of options jumped several decades ago from the financial community into the industrial one through the concept of "real options." The idea here is that instead of buying a financial vehicle a firm buys real assets (hence the "real" in real options) that give it the capability to buy larger capabilities later. The concept first caught on in the energy and commodities sectors, with investing in real assets in oil, gas, copper, and gold (i.e., commodities). Later, the idea evolved into a management strategy focused on providing managerial or project flexibility.

Flexibility comes in several types under the real option concept. One type is the ability to embark on a path very different from the one you are on now. Another theme is the right to invest further through a series of options, by having made the first investment. Note a key difference here from financial options. One can buy a stock option at any time without having made a prior option investment. In the enterprise world however, that is not always the case (as you'll see shortly). Still another type of flexibility is the ability to limit one's losses. If an option does not prove useful, the firm limits its losses mostly to the initial investment while preserving profitability by not having made the full investment in the desired ability.

Let's get concrete to illustrate the types of flexibility. The first and third types of flexibility are evident in the following example. Say you run a ground transport company, and you decide to develop a sea transport capability. Rather than invest in a whole fleet, you can buy two different types of options. You could buy a ship-builder that gives you the later capability to build a fleet. Alternatively, you could buy one or two cargo ships of the type you envision buying later; then use them to learn what you will need to know operationally should you later decide to invest in a larger fleet. Both of these options are less expensive than buying the fleet, so they save money over making the full investment. But that does not mean the options don't have their own payoffs. The options still provide your firm with near-term "returns" in the form of flexibility and insurance (to build a fleet in case you cannot buy one later) or in the form of learning (new skills and capabilities) that speed up the returns from the larger investment.

Stepping back from the concrete to the conceptual, there are seven types of options that you can actively invest in. They are, in order of likeliest usage, options to: accelerate growth, alter firm size, switch inputs, change directions, build nested options, defer investment, and abandon markets.

The growth option generally means the option to accelerate growth, not simply to grow. The underpinnings of this type of option might be purchases of an asset or a capability. An asset option might entail making capital investments in, say, certain computing technology (like grid computing), or in physical plant. A capability option might entail investment in, say, credit risk analysis, that you currently do not have and may not be able to procure later even on an outsourced basis.

The second type of option is the option to alter the operational scale of your firm. This can entail either expansion or contraction options. An expansion option might involve, for example, buying a stake in a much larger manufacturing plant, not currently in your market, but with assets and trained employees that would allow you as a smaller firm to scale into the market as uncertainty resolves. The opposite, a contraction option, might entail selling the right for another firm to buy all of your manufacturing assets should you seek to exit a market or decide that an alternative business form is more profitable.

The third type of option is a switching option. This entails developing the ability to swap in or out the inputs, outputs, or risky assets that you currently use or own. For example, you may purchase substitute materials to see whether products can be made from them. Switching options are not limited to capital assets: they can apply to processes as well. In this example, you might seek to understand new operational processes (in manufacturing or sales) that you do not currently use but that may suddenly become apparent, say, during merger or acquisitions activity.

The fourth type of option is a classic flexibility option. This is the option to change directions. Often this type of option is used to add modularity to current manufacturing capabilities. For example, you might invest in robotic capabilities that allow your firm to produce versions of the same product (say, different color, accessories) from the same manufacturing station.

The fifth type of option is to create staged or nested investments. These are like buying options on options (just to add some complexity to the discussion). The idea here is to create one investment that allows you to invest in follow-on options. Originally developed in the petroleum industry, an option here might entail investing in seismic equipment and analysis capabilities by buying a small consulting firm that later allows you to develop the option of selling mineral rights underneath land you own, or even develop the option to explore for oil itself.

The sixth type of option is the option to defer. This is one of the more complex option types, as investing to defer is often confused with deferring itself. The idea here is to make an investment that defers the primary option or even the main investment until later. An example would be when legal and investment banking services are retained in order to pursue an acquisition that is headed into bankruptcy. Usually, the target is cheaper to purchase out of bankruptcy than before it. So an acquiring firm might pay now to engage in acquisition discussions with the full (hidden) intent of shutting out other potential suitors until the target is forced into bankruptcy.

The final type is the option to abandon. Here you develop an option that will allow you to exit, say, a product line or perhaps even an entire market. Perhaps you have a subsidiary that distracts from a core focus, where the real competition and profitability lie. The real option in this case might be to sell the "right to buy" the division to another firm. Even under options of abandonment, you can capture benefits. You can capture proceeds from abandonment, in this example by selling the "right to buy." And, you can retain the option to re-invest in the same project at a later time.

How Do You Value Real Options?

The two obvious monetary considerations to buying real options are cost and return. With respect to cost, deferring immediate purchase of the ultimate asset or capability does not mean that an option has zero cost. The point, though, is that the option cost makes sense in light of the potential return. In financial markets, option costs are generally lower compared to purchase of the underlying instrument – a stock for example. This is why options are viewed very much like an insurance policy. Indeed, that is an excellent way of viewing them, particularly from the point of view of building real options.

Keeping real options costs low is obviously important because firms still have to show profits. There are a number of ways in which lowered costs are achievable. One is through careful design of the option. Take the shipping fleet example again. Purchasing one or two ships and learning by using them likely has greater payoff, and less risk, than outright buying the shipyard. Owning ships might allow you to develop efficient experiments – another way of lowering option costs – that point to the proper payoff path. Were you then later to enter into a joint venture with the shipyard (rather than buy it outright) then you would be sharing the option cost with a partner, another way of lowering the cost. This, of course, raises alternative risks. In the case of partner-shared costs, one partner may opt to exercise the option at the wrong time for the other.

In the manufacturing sector, there are several additional ways of lowering options costs. Among them, you can test market new products or new advertising messages rather than roll out an expensive campaign. Also, you can prototype different product features to see which ones resonate in the marketplace. Finally, you can leverage new information to change your perceived returns from option exercise, or even to lower the cost of the options itself. For example, you may discover problems in a potential acquisition target that give you leverage to lower the negotiated purchase price.

An important reason for keeping options costs low, aside from the obvious, is the fact that firms may want or need to hedge \ across multiple periods of time. This can mean buying multiple options one after the other. Or it can mean buying options with additional capital required at discrete but potentially unknowable time periods. Take, for example, an export company. It has multiple risk periods in terms of pricing and currency fluctuations. There is the time to produce, the question of when and how much to produce, when to ship, collecting payment, and avoiding currency fluctuations between order and payment. This type of firm would want to buy multiple options (in this case financial more than real) that allow it to realize the profit it desires.

Figuring out whether the firm is one option away from exercise or needs multiple sequential options is not an easy planning exercise. This is because the all-too-common planning method of forecasting current trends forward is going to fail. Instead, the optimal method is to develop and assess future scenarios that might entail one or more option periods and then establish which event in a particular scenario might trigger exercise. Then you have to determine when an option should be purchased. It may well be the case that the purchase date is at a future time that presents risk to the you (i.e., a competitor could purchase the option, say, locking up a key resource). In that case you would want to find yet another option that hedges against that risk. And thus you finds yourself developing sequential hedges that (in this example) could be called compound or nested because of their dependent relationships.

For example, one firm created a compound option out of an enterprise software investment by breaking it into three phases – learning, risk mitigation, and reconfiguration. First the firm invested in analytical capabilities to learn answers to the following key questions. What were the actual benefits to be achieved from the application, and how achievable were they in the abstract? What did firm management have to do in order to achieve those benefits: what changes would be necessary to move from the abstract to the concrete? The learning that accrued from the first option investment led management to understand its internal change management process far better than it had originally thought. Once the benefits were understood, the firm then invested in a second option surrounding risks of the project. Management here invested in research to determine what the riskiest aspects of the project were. Management then had to figure out how to mitigate those risks, and in the process revisit the learning that had occurred in the first phase of the project to determine whether its first-option assessment of benefits still held. Once it was determined that the initial conclusion held, the firm then invested in the third option of the project. In the process, and because of what it had learned from the second option, management reconfigured all the project components so that the lower risk returns were achieved earlier in the software installation and testing cycle.

Even for planning staffs adept at "walking back from the future" to determine when to purchase options, the complex nature of compound options can obscure true value to the firm. This is because returns are often cashless – basic R&D is a classic example – so standard financial tools for evaluating returns fail. Say you are an option-buying firm making staged investments to create alternative launch pads for when you need to react to the market. The costs may be easy enough to understand in this case. The problem is how to value the staged investments, which truth be told, are usually options to spend yet more money. This means avoiding the key methods by which the worth of future projects is traditionally validated. Standard project valuation tools like discounted cash flow (DCF) and net present value (NPV) analyses typically calculate value with simple go / no-go decisions. More importantly, by convention they assign higher hurdle rates for either uncertainty or flexibility and thus lower the project's calculated returns. Real options analysis, by contrast, place increased value on the volatility implied in uncertainty and flexibility. As a result, DCF or NPV analyses usually indicate a project should be avoided when real options analysis may indicate just the opposite.

Another difficulty with standard financial tools is that they tend to stick to a "single path" of analysis. The single-path does not account for interactions of the options across the portfolio. They might, and only might, provide a view of probabilities in the portfolio, but not of the portfolio. This is because the portfolio itself is a unique entity with its own characteristics apart from the projects within it. Those characteristics embody the dependencies, synergies and other interactions of the portfolio contents. Put another way, the projects within a portfolio may be seen as nodes, while the portfolio itself is a system. And as a system, it is subject to its own level of analysis that can prove very insightful. So, for example, NPV analysis might suggest developing one project in the portfolio before another, whereas portfolio analysis might suggest doing the "less-profitable" one first. This is because Project B might actually resolve more uncertainty than Project A. Also, Project B might have a higher variance, which under real options theory would suggest undertaking it first because it has the higher implied value. That same higher variance would be discounted greater by traditional valuation analysis. Moreover, if you appropriately take the portfolio view, by taking the compound option approach the downsides of the higher variance project is limited because the firm still retains the ability to pursue the lower variance project.

Another problem with traditional valuation measures, in this case DCF, is one of time horizon. Looking backward, your firm may not have data going that far back. Looking forward, you may have a very constrained budget horizon, to the point that you may not know if you have the funds to get through most if not the entire period of the uncertainty. Using DCF, you then get stuck trying to forecast resources and needs (revenue, head count, channel mix, prod mix, etc.) because you don't have historical data and you can't fully input assumptions for proper calculating. That makes it difficult for you to engage in forward commitments, such as for contracts, technology purchases, etc. The "seam" between these two time periods – forecast and commitment – can be the source of great friction and uncertainty itself.

The use of traditional financial tools common to most corporate planning processes highlights a larger, strategic problem with the traditional corporate planning process itself. Simply put, planning tools work poorly in the types of market uncertainty we are concerned with here. They simply do not fully capture the options managers have to respond to in an unfolding future. This should not surprise you. After all, our standard valuation tools are based on accounting systems developed for mature enterprises in relatively stable industries. The NPV and DCF methods are not the only ones. Other popular measures such as return on equity (ROE) and return on investment (ROI) can lead firms facing uncertainty into traps of false certainties.

It's human nature to avoid risk and to seek methods that find risk and minimize it. Risk, after all, is normally seen as bad. This is nowhere better reflected than in the higher discount rates used in the NPV and DCF methods. Under real options, by contrast, risk is not automatically a negative event to be avoided. This is because risk, in this case uncertainty can be equated to variance, and variance in financial options drives up the value of an option. The same can be said for real options. Take the shipping fleet example again. The uncertainty is whether you should develop a sea transport fleet. Purchasing the shipyard provides you the option of being able to obtain a fleet. Note that the value is not intrinsic per se. Rather, it is valuable to you, and that is all that matters. Indeed, it may have far less value to counter-parties or competitors (until they begin to understand the larger picture of what you are trying to do). Meanwhile, should you decide after some period of time that you do not want to exercise the option (i.e., to build a fleet) then you can sell the shipyard. Provided the yard is properly run, you might even make a profit from your divestment decision or at the very least break even. The option has provided secondary value in this case, though that may not often be the case, so be careful you don't delude yourself into assuming greater secondary value than what will really be the case.

The concept that conditions of uncertainty can actually drive up value is probably the key insight of the real options approach. The mistake not to make is to assume that an increase in value automatically means the option should be exercised. By the same token, volatility alone is not reason enough for buying options. There are opportunity costs to consider. The rule, derived from option pricing theory, is that you should invest today only if the option value is higher than had you simply waited.

While this may all seem unnecessarily complex, in general this problem should not affect you. Why? Because you should not be making options investments if they are going to lock you into a particular timeframe that is longer than the uncertainty period. That just wouldn't make sense. On the other hand, you should remain vigilant about obvious mistakes. If anything, this discussion hopefully makes you appreciate just how strong a strategy and planning team you better have.

As long as we're on the topic of mistakes, you should understand a couple of other decisions that many firms fail to consider. One is the failure to pull the plug on an option. Just as a financial option can be sold or left to expire, so too can a real option be sold or allowed to expire with no further investment. Effective management of real options requires the mental and managerial rigor to do just that. Too often managers become enamored with an option (because someone's job or bonus depends on it) instead of understanding why it was created. Or, management teams inexperienced in real options confuse delay and value. Taught that value comes from waiting, and that the value of waiting exceeds the value of moving, managers may simply postpone killing an option on the erroneous assumption that further delay further enhances the option value.

Another mistake to avoid is that of confusing rights with resources. Options are simply the right to buy. Just because that right often entails purchasing "resources" does not mean that options are the same thing as resources. They are merely the right to invest further. Paradoxically, then, a real option can entail investing in resources to defer investing in still more resources. No wonder inexperienced management can make the mistake of confusing the two.

If purchasing an option entails purchasing a right, there are also multiple aspects of an option that are helpful to bear in mind. The first aspect to understand and convey to your team the nature of the option, for example a right to develop and commercialize certain technology. Another aspect is the mechanism of the option, for example buying a research and development (R&D) capability. Then comes the cost of the option, which is the investment entailed in developing the R&D capability. Then comes the exercise timing of the option – when you should exercise the right to commercialize. Then there is the exercise price – the actual cost of manufacturing the technology that emanates from the R&D program. Finally, between option purchase and exercise you have to consider the duration of the option. Often this will depend on the competitive environment as much as anything else. For the sake of this example, the firm might want to consider competitors' ability to replicate the option or even to develop substitutes (such as contracting with a design and prototyping firm).

As you might suspect, this last point – option duration, or when to exercise – is one of the most difficult components to assess with real options. Exercise timing is affected by the nature of the option itself, whether it is susceptible to pre-emption; whether it is simple or compound; whether it is proprietary or shared with a partner. If the option is susceptible to pre-emption by competitor actions, that will likely provide a guide to when to exercise or dispose of the option. If the option is simple, meaning that after one option investment the next decision is to make the full investment, then you will have one timing decision. However, if the option is compound, meaning that the option investment needs to be followed by another one or more before the final investment is made, then you face the difficulty of having to "walk back" from the future investment date to determine when you should make the intervening investments. If the option is shared with a partner, then exercise timing may not be entirely under your control; a partner sharing in the option may force the decision based on its own needs.

Criticism of the Real Options Approach

The perceived, if not outright, complexity of real options portfolio strategy has attracted criticism over inevitable gaps in logic. Much of the criticism is what one might call "tactical" in nature. Compared to the other two major strategies discussed previously, the strategic value of hedging with real options is difficult to negate. But the criticism merits attention if for no other reason than it can help you build still better portfolios of options.

The most basic criticism is that of using real options at all, that there is real loss from deferring the larger investment. That is, if the firm holds an option and does not exercise it to buy the asset, then the firm loses the "dividend" that the asset may have been paying out. In the shipping transport example, if the firm opts to purchase boats and never buys the shipyard, it may be missing the profits from the yard's operations that might have funded other projects, options, and so forth.

A separate vein of criticism focuses on the thorny problem of valuation. Critics claim that valuation all too often seems like a "know it when you see it" construct. Critics say this is particularly true when investing in intangible assets (like design capabilities), where "valuation" appears to be based on the decisions that occur after the acquisition of the intangible asset or capability. Perhaps the criticism carries weight because the rationale is often provided after the fact. Fair enough. But it is not necessarily the case that value cannot be discerned before the fact. Sophisticated quantitative analysis (like dynamic programming, or carefully framed binomial option pricing models) can be used to test the insights and conclusions developed during the qualitative assessment process.

What the criticism really points out is the need to pay attention to making all options costs tangible. Particular costs to watch out for are opportunity costs

– what you would have done had you not invested in the option, and what you do once you have. For example, if you have an environmental-related option, you may have to devote staff or staff time to responding to new regulatory requirements, such as updating environmental impact statements on a regular basis. Other costs to bear in mind include end-point costs. For example, in abandoning the shipping option, salvage costs may be higher than what you originally estimated. This can happen, for example, if you are adversely negotiated against (or even lied to) during the original bidding process. In exercising the option, there may be cost over-runs because, for example, resource prices (like fuel!) rise dramatically and unexpectedly.

Another criticism of the real options portfolio approach focuses on mis-measuring volatility and thus falsely raising the perceived value of an option. This error can result from problematic data. Data measured across one timeframe may overstate volatility than when measured across a different timeframe. For example, you may have good quarterly data but have to make exercise decisions on a day-to-day basis. Measured daily, the data may demonstrate a greater level of volatility than the quarterly data show. You then risk imputing higher value to the option (because of the high daily volatility) than what is truly warranted, and thus pay too much for it or (more likely) exercise too early.

Another criticism stems from the ill-understood nature of systemic interactions between options in a portfolio set, and the costs – financial and otherwise –

that building the wrong portfolio can incur. Building a large options portfolio obviously can be financially expensive. It can also serve to dilute or divert the focus of your management. The end result is that you do not anticipate costs, value, or exercise time appropriately and lose the value of the option. As noted earlier, to the extent that options interact, they can not only increase overall portfolio value but they ca also lower it more than the aggregate value of individual options would otherwise suggest. Building big portfolios thus risk value dilution. You can maintain that value, however, with an aggressive abandonment strategy – even to the point of building abandonment options on top of your options.

Assuming for the moment that you put together an optimal portfolio where the options values blend systemically in the portfolio: that does not mean that they will continue to do so once exercise begins on the first one. Exercising one option, for example, might stimulate a competitor to act. In turn, that might drive up the value of a different option or force you to exercise sooner than anticipated. Both of these situations are indicative of higher volatility, which theoretically would increase option value. You have to be aware that the portfolio can experience lower value because of the reactions that exercising options stimulates. This is why you need to take into account possible competitor reactions to each option – and the impact on others – as you assemble your portfolio. This may feel like a chess game where success is determined by thinking ahead several moves for each of your opponents' potential actions. Good portfolio builders are used to thinking this way, suggesting that you want one on your strategy and planning team.

Critics have also identified several dilemmas you face when trying to exercise options related to technology. One is the dilemma of the unexpectedly high exercise price, or even a moderate escalation of price. Simple internal politics can cause this. One of your managers may seek to stave off perceived damage to their competency, particularly if it affects their "empire." They may even sabotage exercising the option by promoting further investment in their own particular area. Conversely, your managers may be too weak to help exercise options. They may not have the political or social capital to help kill standard operating routines, thereby escalating exercise costs to the firm. Other managers, in a misguided spirit of cost-cutting, may refuse to allow necessary parallel investment.

So in addition to option complexity, you have to take into account good old-fashioned corporate politics. For good or bad, option exercise can be highly influenced by firm "champions" and their track record for success. This can work to the advantage of the firm under conditions of uncertainty when a strong champion favors exercise. They may be able to get a low-cost exercise approved with little interference. By contrast, a weak champion might get a high-cost exercise rejected with little review. Naturally, a strong champion can derail exercise if it conflicts with their personal agenda. But so can a weak champion by taking advantage of the more collective nature of decisions within a firm, they can create alliances that derail exercise by death of a thousand "buts."

Personal agendas aside, there are organizational pressures, too. If an option is organizationally integrated into firm operations, there may be strong pressure for success because of the visibility of the option. This can create unhealthy bias in favor of the option. If uncertainty remains high, the option may become too difficult to abandon and may continue indefinitely, never contributing the intended value. In the same vein, pressure for success may encourage firms to exercise options on poor investments (i.e., not keep the option going but actually exercise it). A defense contractor, for example, may fail to kill a weapon system that doesn't meet future battlefield needs because it does meet the current pipeline timeline for production and delivery. Overcoming such bias may require a new management team or shuffling the one you have to make it strong enough to withstand abandoning an option.

If strong organizational integration can be a problem, so too can isolation from the firm. Some firms opt to create new organizational structures to isolate pilot projects (options) from main operations. When that happens, you risk exhibiting bias against options exercise because the option knowledge gained may be considered "experimental." Xerox provides a classic example of this dilemma. Through its PARC technology laboratory, Xerox developed some of the most innovative – and commonly used – software and hardware technology for the personal computer. Two examples are the mouse and the graphical user interface (GUI). However, Xerox failed to capitalize on these two innovations because they were isolated by the firm's perceived core competencies in marketing and xerography. To add insult to injury, they are now a second player to other players in the very area where they thought they held their competencies.

Another example comes from GM's Saturn division. Saturn represented an option on changing the culture at GM. It succeeded to the extent that Saturn was able to create a team culture non-existent elsewhere within GM. It was a failure because that team culture could not be integrated with the rest of the firm and the prevailing one proved too strong. GM had to kill Saturn or let it wither on the vine (the direction it ultimately chose) even as it moved simultaneously to create integrated divisions espousing the same culture.

Finally, Monsanto's entry into the biotechnology industry demonstrates what sometimes has to happen to overcome integration resistance. In Monsanto's case it was initially unable to integrate its biotechnology assets because its core chemical business line had different routines and even research approaches. The chemical line was more mature, was beyond basic R&D, and as such required much tighter integration with customers. The biotech business, by contrast, required more basic research to create potential products. Ultimately Monsanto had to spin off its core chemical business in order to exercise the biotech option.

In the portfolio context, problems of isolation and integration can be magnified. Say you create a portfolio of options on the assumption that you can abandon some later. If integrated, too many options risks creating political constituencies inside the firm dependent upon certain options for success, in turn inadvertently driving the exercise of too many options. Exercising all those options could bleed your firm dry. By the same token, isolating them risks raising the organizational costs of duplicating staffing and resources,– again instituting a drain on profitability. Recall from earlier that such inefficiencies are often the price of creating flexibility. Duplicating staff may be necessary investment in the short run. Just go into it with your eyes wide open, and make sure you keep the green-eyeshade guys aware of why the duplicate investment is being made.

If the basic dilemma you face is that integration raises the risk of undertaking a bad option and isolation raises the risk of killing a good one, then external review can be one solution for mitigating these risks. Say you prefer integration over isolation, you can then use outsiders with minimal or little political capital in the firm in order to evaluate whether you should exercise or not. Advisory boards are perfect for this sort of thing. Since many firms use them for other oversight functions already, implementing such a Board should not be difficult. Advisory board members, though, should not be used simply to evaluate option purchase or exercise. They should be used also to vet the internal decision-making process of your firm. That way you have a check on the larger question of whether you are implementing an effective options strategy and portfolio.

In particular, there are three areas of internal processes that advisory boards could be encouraged to review. One area involves the errors caused by extrapolating from the past to the future. For example, routines that are successful in ongoing operations tend to be retained (why toss what works?). These routines are then applied to new situations whether warranted or not. This creates competency traps whereby new routines are rejected as contrary to current competencies. Current success effectively crowds out the incentive or willingness to adopt new routines. Monsanto faced this in the example discussed previously, and took rather drastic steps. Instead, a strong advisory board might have helped the firm maneuver within the cultural conflict and retain both business lines.

Another area where advisory boards can help is in avoiding other cognitive biases. The creation of options is fraught with all kinds of biases. For example, people tend to reject information that questions their current assumptions. They underrate the probability or consequences of negative information. Their judgments on revenues and costs are consequently likely to be significantly skewed (i.e. estimating bias). You or your management may be over confident and attribute success to your own actions or superior ability and attribute failures to external events. Your team may naturally assume failure is a bad thing. Managers acting this way will seek to avoid failure, often trying to reduce turbulence, or volatility, in the firm. In the process, your team may paradoxically reduce the value of the options that could actually keep your firm alive in the new market that emerges. A good advisory board can help management see and avoid these mistakes.

Some Attributes of Hedgers

Companies that build hedging portfolios tend to leverage variety, certain cultural characteristics, and possibly size to build competitive advantage. Variety is a lever in that it is not just a result from building an options portfolio, but it also is a competitive weapon in and of itself. Honda's rise to prominence over Yamaha in the motorcycle market is a case in point. Yamaha was the dominant Japanese player in the US market for long after Honda's initial entry. Honda changed the dynamic when it began introducing variety in the form of improvements and then features at a pace faster than Yamaha could respond. Whereas Yamaha had the competency in engine production, and on that basis built a reputation for higher powered cycles, Honda redefined its competencies to that of having faster design-to-market production and began building a reputation for meeting consumer preferences better than Yamaha did.

In terms of characteristics that help define a successful portfolio builder, there are many typically found together. For starters, hedgers understand the importance of accepting and embracing the uncertainty. As such, you should display a preference for valuing flexibility over adherence to rules or standard operating procedures. In your planning methods, you should embrace what-if questioning and scenario building over classic planning processes that auto-pilot future investment.

Following from that, you should accept that planning may produce an initiative process guided more by objectives than by delineated tasks or projects. This in turn means having more of an investment philosophy and approach to budgetary allocation than the bean-counting approach typical of accountants. There may not even be strict budgets per se. You may decide to carve off large parts of retained earnings for option investment governed at the corporate versus the division level. You may even opt to manage and budget by objective rather than organization, difficult as this can become as your firm increases in size. One of those objectives should include a focus on budgeting for knowledge development – such as through market intelligence acquisition – instead of the more common asset-based approach that informs typical corporate planning.

Leaders of successful hedging firms exhibit unique personal characteristics as well. For example, they tend to be highly analytical, using evidence-based decision-making, rather than intuiting from what has worked in the past. They also stay extremely focused over long periods of time, preferring planning horizons that span beyond a year to perhaps four or five years. While this may seem contradictory to being highly focused, longer planning horizons let smart hedgers be more flexible than their typical corporate counterparts who become set in their adherence to plans. Similarly, highly analytical as they may be, hedgers also respect the role and rate of error in their work. They tolerate failure. They appreciate that the longer out the time horizon, the more likely forecasting errors are to arise. Consequently, these leaders often do not invest themselves in doing things the traditional way, but prefer being more conceptual and valuing the gathering of knowledge. This is why more data-oriented colleagues like market researchers and finance staff often make better leaders than do line managers in a hedging firm.

To close out this topic, the issue of whether size is an effective lever for hedging remains an open question. The idea here is that building an options portfolio can require sizeable investment, and this is best supported by larger firms. Also, larger firms tend to have more "slack," so some part of them can focus on the change process. Certainly slack allows for experimentation, which supports the real options approach. In order to create or protect that slack you would be wise to become a steward of slack resources so that they are not immediately reassigned to someone's pet project.

How Hedgers Win

Hedging firms succeed for a number of reasons, chief among them being that their strategy blends some of the better aspects of the pioneer and pouncer strategies. For example, hedging provides you the opportunity to choose when to make your commitment, which allows you to act like a pioneer while building flexibility like a pouncer. The ability to delay commitment has been discussed already. But the opposite is important to understand as well. Real options can help you to "fail fast." They can help you make decisions to exit a market faster than otherwise would have been the case, saving you high costs associated with continuation in that same market. By investing in options that can cause "failure," you can gain intermediate, not just long term, value. This is because even options that fail enhance your accumulated resource and knowledge base. They can help reduce uncertainty. They can increase variety or flexibility. They can stimulate the search for new opportunities, either in new markets or even by creating a converging ones. Convergence need not be just product oriented (e.g., smart phones), it can be operational as well. Early phone companies typically ran their landline and wireless capabilities as separate businesses. With option investments made in backbone technologies and organization, those same firms now reap the benefits of operational integration that, with the help of the internet, now extends to the retail interface with the customer as well. This integration may seem obvious in hindsight. But the telcos had to engage in some very novel thinking to get to this point.

By hedging, you can leverage more than one option in your portfolio, allowing you to create a greater mix of products or services than can your competitors. This mix may then begin to drive customer preferences, giving you the opportunity to dominate over your competitors. An example of this comes from Microsoft. That firm saw an advantage to developing and / or buying firms that made different pieces of software that Microsoft could link into its own operating system software (its original product base). Combining key software modules – word processing, spreadsheet, and presentation – into the Office suite drove customer preferences first in the corporate then in the consumer world. No longer did software buyers have to worry about software conflicts, especially as Microsoft embarked on a strategy of making it more difficult for third party software providers to link easily into its operating system.

Staying on the competitive theme for a moment, another reason you can succeed as a hedger is that options give you the opportunity to influence your competitors in ways that pouncers generally cannot, and that pioneers do not unless they make a big bet. Hedgers can preemptively move to drive down the value of rivals' options. You can even pre-empt by making a small commitment – not the large one of a pioneer – and thereby spoof a competitor into making a larger commitment or exercising options it otherwise would not. For example, you can signal intent to enter a market, even though you do not intend to, in order to bluff your rival into exercising their own entry. Forcing rivals' hands this way causes those rivals to forfeit the value of their own options two ways; by forcing further investment and by taking away the value of waiting.

As a hedger you can also compete by publicly making options investments, the exercise of which would drive down the value or nullify competitor investments. A great example here is the Strategic Defense Initiative started in the early 1980's. Decades later, does it exist? No. Does any part of it exist? Hardly. The option was never exercised, and no matter the reason why, it achieved the intended goal. That goal was to convince the Soviet Union that its mobile missile modernization program – ahead of the United States at the time – was not worth further investment. The goal was to convince the Soviet Union that they needed their own defensive program, which by the way would be very, very expensive. Our option, by driving down the Soviet's perception of the value of their mobile missiles caused our Cold War competitor to seek to invest in the exact same option. In so doing, the Soviets further bankrupted themselves, leading to their collapse.

Finally, another competitive advantage from hedging strategy is that it can be a launching pad for engaging in one of the other strategies. Options centered on partnering, for example, can allow you to enter a market like a pioneer through joint ventures or alliances. Alternatively, hedging can give you time to enter markets, allowing you to take on a pouncer strategy as necessary.

How Hedgers Lose

Of course, not all hedgers win, and there are legitimate reasons why that occurs. In a snapshot, there is a lot more you have to get right than what you have to do as a first or pouncer. A key problem, for example, is determining what to hedge against. You can obviously hedge against a key market uncertainty. Or you can hedge your current investment paths. Hopefully these converge, but it's fair to assume that often they do not. Or, take the case of compound hedges. The right set has to be identified. Then you have to figure out how to put on the hedge right, and in the right order. Say you get the structure of the hedge right. You can still lose on timing the entry or exercise wrong. Good firms can train to get the nature of the hedge right, even complex ones. That said, you still cannot easily identify when to exercise an option. Layer in compound options and the complexity of execution grows significantly. To get this right you need a very strong scenario-based planning methodology. Such methods require staff well-trained in walking back from future scenarios (the ones to hedge in case they occur) and identifying the path, milestones, and signposts that indicate when such divergences occur.

All of the above is predicated on your own internal actions. Now consider your competitive environment. If timing hedge entry and exit is difficult enough in a vacuum, competitors have a very nasty habit of forcing change at unwanted times. Rival firms can pre-empt in the marketplace in ways that increase the costs of your options, their execution, and even change their type. For example, a government can commit to a large-scale program to build relatively short-range tactical jet fighters (like the F-22). An enemy can then invest asymmetrically in missiles to strike any air or sea port to beyond the fighters' fuel capacity. Now the government is forced to examine a range of new, potentially expensive options (such as building more long-range re-fuelers), as well as the difficult decision of whether to divest (expensively) from a new program.

Expensive divestment raises another difficulty of hedging strategies. By now, you should be aware that you will be less efficient when you invest in options that do not contribute directly – either through new revenues or operational efficiencies – to the bottom line. For public firms, this inefficiency is usually picked up by Wall Street analysts through crude measures like G&A or cost margins, who then compare you to non-hedging (and therefore lower cost) competitors. Your stock then suffers compared to where it would be without the perceived inefficiency, and it suffers compared to rivals. What this suggests is that hedging firms have to ignore the pressure of Wall Street – Microsoft's and Apple's typical stance – or develop some way of communicating the fact that the firm is hedging without giving away the hedge. Of course, doing so eliminates the strategic surprise of the hedge, but that may be a necessary sacrifice if the firm cannot shrug off the short-term pressures of Wall Street.

In addition to financial inefficiencies, hedging firms also suffer organizational inefficiencies that can dilute or mitigate success. For example, you may not fully exploit an option because you actually think you will divest yourself of it. Corporate politics being what it is, your management team may not be willing to be associated with a "losing" program. If the options or hedges are managed separately from the main operations of the firm, then you will likely have to duplicate organizations, increasing managerial complexity. If the options or hedges are not managed separately from the firm, then you risk utterly confusing middle management as to what is core and what is the hedge. And once you've confused middle management, you are more likely to fail overall in executing on your core firm activities.

If the hedge involves alternative product designs, presumably even competing designs, then you will create market inefficiencies for the firm. Competing designs may require duplicate investment in advertising, promotion, endorsement, distribution channels, input materials, etc. Your sales force may have a lower commitment to one particular design (the lower selling one usually). Piloting sales of the new design can create confusion among your customers. At least one of your products is going to be less desirable than the other(s) for a variety of reasons. Nevertheless, sales of the least desirable one in turn could slow down or cannibalize market share growth of the dominant one, confusing your own firm as well. The company brand risks being diluted, cutting into all sales. Under stress, rivalry within your firm can increase. Managers may start to use their power to win "battles," pushing your firm into a less competitive or less efficient posture.

A Final Thought

Viewed in this light, you may rightly wonder why hedge. Here's why. The potential failures of hedges are not unique. You can fail in many of the same ways in the course of normal investment. You can get the timing wrong. You can create inefficiencies (or the perception of them) that investors punish. You can confuse internal managers. And you can confuse customers: the ultimate no-no. Indeed, substitute the word "operations" for "hedges" and clearly the same failures can strike non-hedging firms as well. But in those cases, you've not created a better opportunity to manage the uncertainty you face. And you may have wasted even greater resources than had you invested in one or more hedges (especially real options).

Take a look around your own firm. You can probably find a few examples. The landscape is littered with firms that failed on the basics, and we're not just talking start-ups here (e.g. GM). So at this point, armed with what you've learned thus far, the next step is to learn how you can assess the three strategies to achieve success at the lowest cost and the lowest comparative risk that is tolerable to your firm – a topic to which we now turn.

6 STRATEGY SELECTION

Successfully navigating uncertainty means selecting and implementing the right strategy. The prior chapters described three primary strategies you can use when in such periods of uncertainty. The strategies, however, are not cookie-cutter, one-size-fits-all. Yes, we've discussed in general terms the types of firms that may opt for one strategy over another. But in reality, there is all kinds of internal information that should inform your decision.

In selecting your strategy, you should be asking yourself a number of practical questions. To help you do so, this final chapter will focus on providing a framework for what you should evaluate as you go about that task. This framework will focus on the impact of failure; the importance of differentiation; the impact of market dynamism; management's role;

organizing for the strategy; and competitively shifting among the strategies.

The Impact of Failure

Fear of failure is clearly an impetus for undertaking bold strategy under periods of uncertainty. But are all failures the same, or is their impact the same? The two most serious forms of failure you should focus on are the failure to survive and failure to dominate the market. Clearly, your firm can survive and yet not dominate the market. You might shrink and occupy a market niche and successfully stay there for a long time, generating decent returns on capital once you have shrunk to your new, sustainable size. (The American auto makers have been headed down this path for some time now.) Clearly this has involved an erosion of existing shareholder value, yet new shareholders can still enter and potentially profit. The point is, be open to thinking about failure in relative, not absolute, terms.

From there, consider whether there are different types of failure for each strategy. (The short answer is that some failures are the same, and others unique.) To recap an earlier discussion, pioneers can fail to identify the right move; they can get timing wrong; they can create inefficiencies, particularly with "big bets;" and they can confuse their own management and customers. What about for pouncers? The answer is: their failures can be the same. Hedgers can create inefficiencies like the others, but otherwise their failures are generally different by nature of the strategy. They may get exercise timing wrong (not market entry timing, but pre-market investment). They may fail to put on a compound hedge in the right order. They may fail to kill a hedge.

Where the types of failures may be similar, you should consider that the magnitude of failure may be different for the different strategies or the probabilities of failure may be different. And these differences not only matter, but their probability or impact in your particular circumstances should help define which strategy you choose. For example, in the pouncer strategy, you may generate far greater internal inefficiencies because of the organizational nature of investment called for under pouncer strategy. Compare this to the more partial investment approach of a real option under a hedging strategy. Even if a hedging strategy risks wrong timing on investment, or risks confusing internal stakeholders, the magnitude of failure may not be as great if your investments are lower than what they would have been had you pursued one of the other two strategies. In this case, such lower investments may leave you with enough slack capital to invest in a crash survival gambit even if your hedging strategy fails, and certainly compared to taking on a big bet as a pioneer.

The Importance of Differentiation

The second element of the framework to consider is how much each strategy differentiates you from the competition. Of course, for any given strategy there are some easy actions that can promote diversity no matter which is chosen. For example, you can form alliances with very different partners (either within the company's value chain, or preferably outside). You can expand or re-compose Boards with very different directors than those currently in position. As a somewhat less extreme approach (perhaps given the valued connections of various board members), you may want to consider creating boards of advisors to mitigate the dangers of group-think.

How should you begin thinking about differentiating? Well, you can start by identifying and acquiring very different personnel. What you want to do is embed new knowledge in the "system" of personnel rather than in select or key personnel (like the way food companies split recipes among more than one person). Without even hiring, you can develop one or more decentralized, cross-functional, teams to review and facilitate continuous resource improvement and reduce conformity. Of course, you can also always hire consultants.

Take care here, though. If your firm begins to shed workers for some unforeseen reason, you may find your valuable knowledge and practices spread to your rivals in the industry. If you hire consultants, avoid the tendency to cover your posterior by hiring the name brand firms. There are only a few, and since they work with so many of the same large firms, they unwittingly spread the same business models around, making it difficult to differentiate. What you can do is hire one of the larger consulting firms to develop a benchmarking study since they will already be very familiar with the sector from their other clients. The point here is to understand what to avoid. If your competitors in the sector have one particular set of benchmarks then they are likely imitating each other. That's good for you to know. You can now evaluate to what extent each strategy will help create alternative practices or benchmarks for the future environment rather than the current one.

The Impact of Market Dynamism

Market dynamism can impact strategy execution to the point of influencing which strategy you should select. When selecting a strategy for low to moderately dynamic markets – where change may be frequent, but roughly predictable and linear – you might want to consider a more structured and analytic process for managing execution. This might cause you to lean in favor of a portfolio strategy. In hyper-dynamic markets, by contrast, you may be too stressed to "learn by doing." The firm will need much simpler strategy routines and avoid the complex. This may be as simple as maintaining a list of "priorities," or a few simple "rules." For example, Yahoo has maintained only two rules in the hyper-dynamic world of alliance building among internet firms. First, no alliance can be exclusive. Second, no alliance can violate the business model of keeping the basic service free to users. Done well like this, simple routines can provide enough structure to guide execution. They also suggest that you might favor analytically less complex strategies like those for the pioneer or pouncer.

Sometimes, though, routines will not provide "sufficient" guidance amidst the market chaos. And you have to consider the role of mistakes. Most readers may know the story about Edison not firing a subordinate who had just committed a six-figure error (large for the time). In saving the subordinate's neck, Edison is supposed to have said that he just paid a fortune for that man's education not to make the same mistake again. Alas, Edison's insight about human learning is not the norm today. Take the military for example. In its current leadership selection process, one mistake often nixes a colonel or captain for elevation to the general or admiral corps. Never mind the fact that the officer may be the best leader for an emerging form of warfare. The system de facto has become to select the best leader for the current environment (which tolerates no mistakes). Corporate intolerance for mistakes is only slightly less severe. Large mistakes engender a defensiveness that hinders learning (the CYA effect). You walk a fine line here; mistakes can create learning so long as they are not so large that they trigger rationalization (and thus suppress learning from the mistake).

When routines do not provide the guidance you need, you should focus on creating new, specific knowledge. This could involve, for example, conducting experiments or pilot projects to stimulate new learning. Pioneers often do precisely this, and it is one of the key advantages associated with that strategy. The experimenter accepts small losses for immediate feedback. As the learning increases, the firm then cycles back to traditional, more linear planning processes for exploring market alternatives.

What you have to consider when experimenting is the longer-term downside. The most obvious is cost and the potential loss of limited capital if the experiments are unsuccessful. Those you have probably already considered. There are others that merit greater attention on your part. For example, the more dynamic the market, the higher the probability that learning gained from experiments will be lost due to high turn-over among job-hopping personnel. Also, if sloppily managed, experimentation can slip too easily into unstructured operations, pushing a division or even an entire firm near chaos. The challenge is to manage the organizational structure so as not to lose newly-developed capabilities in the context of a high-velocity environment. In less dynamic markets, this should be less of a concern. Here, competitive advantage typically is destroyed by external forces. In hyper-dynamic markets, by contrast, competitive advantages can be destroyed internally by the collapse of structure and routine. Determining which market environment predominates, then, becomes a key element of strategic preparation and strategy selection.

The Role of Management

Another element to consider in the framework is the role of management. There are two main ways you can play your role most effectively. The first is to see the environmental changes and adjust the firm's culture accordingly. As a senior leader you have the right to upset preconceptions about corporate direction or even question the organization's culture. By modifying compensation, scorecard measures, and management organization you can instill new routines that change with the environment.

The second is to effect change through the control of firm resources. If the goal is to create new capabilities, especially ones that cross functions, then you have to be the strategy champion. This is because internal accounting and finance units usually have too much of a quarterly focus to see the strategic nature of key investments on their own. Even strategic business unit heads can have difficulty making strategic investments. This situation arises when resources are needed from elsewhere, principally other SBU heads. In such cases, only the corporate head can protect those from whom he raids resources in order to serve the more over-arching corporate strategy. The raided unit's performance will likely degrade with divestment. Unit management may accordingly feel they cannot or will not be promoted. So, in the absence of higher level intervention, lower tier managers often wage fierce battles to prevent resource raiding.

Now, in an ideal world, senior leaders would see the wisdom of not penalizing those who sacrifice for the good of the company. This is where transparency becomes so important. As long as progress is made visible and accountability maintained, there should be few "losers" in a given transformation process. A unit head may lose investment but gain personally (through stock and options grants) with company-wide success. This, then, becomes your role – to adjudicate resource flows and protect those who may be perceived as losing but are really sacrificing for the good of the overall firm.

Organizing for the Strategy

Realistically speaking, adopting any new strategy suggests that some form of organizational change is likely. After all, your firm is theoretically already organized correctly to execute the current strategy, not a new one. So when you develop new strategic options – be it as a pioneer, pouncer, or hedger – then you will likely want to focus on two process paths. One involves developing procedures for expanding your firm's knowledge of new markets and market behaviors. For example, you may need to develop new market research or new competitive intelligence capabilities in order not to miss seeing competitor moves. The other involves developing procedures to expand company capabilities. For example, you might consider breaking apart your budgeting and procurement process into smaller, discretely funded elements. Initiative budgeting might be broken down to design, pre-construction, construction, experimentation, and commercialization phases. This not only gives you greater insight into where you are in the capabilities development process, but it allows for quicker divestment should that become necessary. Similarly, a hedger could create a "real options" team separate from the normal strategic planning cell. A pioneer could create a separate exploratory "big bet" team, though that team would sooner rather than later have to be melded into the normal strategic process so the firm does not lose focus.

On a related note, you will also have to consider the implications of pursuing different options in more than one sub-unit. One decision could have an impact on multiple entrepreneurial activities, and that may not be a good thing. To the extent possible, independent options should be placed in organizations such that they don't affect each other. That way the fate of each – exercise, further investment, or divestment – can be decided independently without diminishing the value of the overall portfolio.

The flip side of creating new units to develop new capabilities is integrating units to do the same. There are two main times when you might consider doing so. The first is when a sub-unit is being re-integrated into the firm in order to begin using the newly developed capability. The second is when the new capability is actually being developed from a combination of units. An excellent study by Michael Raynor of Deloitte Consulting illustrates the point. Writing about Sprint in the context of real options investment, Raynor noted that Sprint's big growth past the old-line telephony firms occurred as a result of several capabilities it developed by combining unit product lines. In this case, Sprint management dynamically linked three key divisions – local telephony, consumer and business services, and wireless – overlaying a new joint marketing team and a common organizational architecture. The result was the discovery that long-distance being sold over land lines at five cents per minute could instead be re-packaged and sold to wireless customers for ten cents a minute. Sprint effectively doubled its per-minute revenue using the same physical infrastructure.

Sprint did not end its real options experimentation with that success. Instead it pushed a real options philosophy into the firm's ongoing way of doing business. According to Raynor, Sprint focused on being able to re-configure its divisional linkages rapidly and frequently. To do so, all major divisions began reporting directly to the COO. No layer of executives existed between the operating units and the corporate office. This also minimized the development of strong fiefdoms. Meanwhile, Sprint changed its rewards structure to better align the divisions behind new efforts as well as to reward cooperative behavior by divisional managers.

Contrast Sprint's treatment of organizational structure with that of a pioneer. In the latter, a very different organizational approach – one might say autocratic – may be necessary. The pioneer will need to force tight alignment around corporate objectives. This is particularly true for pioneers making big bets, since they will need tighter control over execution than that suggested by Sprint's case. Meanwhile, as the future path becomes set, strategic planning reverts back to a traditional bottom-up initiative process with its tendency to suppress distracting activities. Compensation becomes formulaically tied to initiatives as they become more concrete in order to reinforce the selected path of the firm.

MASTERING UNCERTAINTY

If tighter hierarchical integration makes sense for a pioneer, why is it often true for pouncers too? Well, pouncers need to develop the ability to maneuver quickly in the market in order to overtake pioneers. If the measure of success is time, then an argument can be made that tighter integration achieves faster execution times. If initiatives are not centrally integrated, they might create idiosyncratic behavior in some part(s) of the firm. And, any idiosyncrasy is likely to have a negative, not positive, impact on speed of movement. Outsourcing may be an organizational exception to this idea of tighter integration. This is because outsourcing certain legacy functions may allow the pouncer to divest of them faster as it embarks on its new path.

Competitively Shifting Strategy

Before we close out the discussion, there is one final issue to consider – that of shifting strategy mid-course. The beauty of the strategies presented here is that pursuing one does not mean that another is off the table. In the same market competition you can pursue one strategy and then switch to another to enhance your competitive standing. The key questions are what might influence your decision to switch strategies and what are the possible repercussions from doing so.

So, for example, you can pursue a hedging strategy and, as the uncertainty clears, switch to a pioneer strategy. That would allow you to shape competitor perceptions of the market and drive them into spending behavior detrimental to their success. The same may be true for being a pouncer as well. You may gain a window of opportunity to switch to a pioneer strategy and drive the emergence of the "dominant design,".

Hedgers have the most flexibility in terms of switching strategies. Theoretically, a hedger may even be able to switch to both other strategies at the same time. While not a hedger in the way this book has defined them, Apple nonetheless provides a great recent example, engaging in both pioneer and pouncer strategies at the expense of its rivals. Apple was clearly a pouncer in the digital audio player market with its iPod, leveraging design to kill off the pioneers. But it was also a legitimate pioneer in the online music market with the launch of iTunes. By marrying its pioneer advantage in one area (iTunes) with its late mover status in another (iPods), Apple was able to establish dominance over the online music business in a way no other firm has been able to match to date.

There can be strong reasons for switching out of a hedging strategy. For example, you may need to expose some of your own investments in order to prompt rivals to provide key competitive intelligence unwittingly. Or, preemptively exercising a compound option may provide you access to scarce resources needed for the next investment stage. Worse, you may need to give up diversifying simply because of insufficient funds. Finally, you may determine that late market entry is not feasible and so need to change the basis for competition. This can occur, for example, when unexpected patents emerge. You may decide to pre-empt in the market place in order to deny the patent-holding firm the opportunity to lock you out.

There are a number of other influences that could shape your decision to switch strategies. One is market size, along with competitive posture, changing risk assessments, and finally the determination of whether flexibility or focus is needed at the point of market entry. With respect to size, anticipated revenues or market share influence whether a hedger switches to a pioneer or pouncer strategy. For example, if the market size is small, then you may opt to switch to a pioneer strategy to capture the most market share. If market size is large, you can afford to adopt a pouncer strategy to take advantage of pioneer mistakes. The underlying logic here centers on learning opportunities. The more learning that needs to be done, the more likely a firm will switch into a pouncer strategy. By the same token, the less learning left to be done, then the more likely you will want to switch to a pioneer strategy to leverage that learning and deny opportunity for others to learn it as well.

Competitive posturing is another influence on strategy shifts. The more unique an input resource, for example, the more likely you will want to switch to a pioneer strategy. You will want to lock up the resource to deny it to your competitors. Resource durability will also affect the direction of strategy switching. The less durable a necessary resource, the more likely you want to switch to a pioneer strategy so you can take advantage of it before it is lost (and vice versa).

Risk assessment also plays a role in strategy switching. This is somewhat of a technical discussion, but it is important. You may want to come back to it again to absorb the lesson. The central concept here is the risk / reward relationship. As you may recall from the prior chapter, most planning staffs use NPV or DCF functions to evaluate potential investment returns. Embedded in those functions is a "hurdle" rate, or the percent return a project has to yield to be worth investing. Each firm has its own hurdle rate. That rate is usually reflective of another rate implicitly embedded – a risk-free rate. Suffice to say that, generally speaking, the lower the risk-free rate, the lower the hurdle rate you need to make in order to be profitable to your shareholders.

By extension, the lower the hurdle rate, the more likely you can afford to switch to a pioneer strategy. For example, if you are a pioneer that has to incur extra costs to educate the market to accept your design, then you would expect your initial returns to be low. But if the hurdle rate is low, you can still be profitable even when making mistakes.

In contrast, if the hurdle rate is high, then your initial market returns may be less profitable. This could lead you to switch to a pouncer strategy. That way you can await the development of efficiencies, drive down your internal costs, and thus be better positioned for profitable market entry even on lower margins. Or, a high hurdle rate might suggest a high price for making mistakes in the marketplace. This could lead you to switch from a first or pouncer strategy to a hedging one. The idea would be that you need to develop hedges to mitigate the price of potential market mistakes. You also might switch to a hedging strategy in order to seek higher-margin opportunities, possibly even in unrelated markets.

Finally, the last influence on switching strategies is the decision of choosing either flexibility or focus. To the extent that focus is required to dominate the market upon entry (true for small markets), then you would want to switch to a pioneer strategy or (perhaps in a larger market) possibly a pouncer one. However, there could be instances where you are pursuing a focused path and suddenly realize the uncertainty is going to last longer than you anticipated – say if you see a pioneer fail significantly. In that case, you might switch over to a hedging strategy, giving up focus in exchange for building flexibility.

At this point, perhaps a warning is in order. There are social views of risk that can cause bad decisions. In particular, you have to be aware of the natural fear of uncertainty that most people have. It's hard-wired into us. Here's the potential problem: You understand (hopefully) by now that you can mitigate gross uncertainty with a hedging strategy. But that doesn't make the uncertainty go away. So what can happen is that the fear of uncertainty triggers an early reaction, and you begin to commit when you should remain flexible. At its worst, that fear may induce gambling – making a big bet and effectively becoming a pioneer. Or you may switch to a pioneer strategy falsely believing you are resolving the uncertainty – the "At least I'm doing something" strategy. Never underestimate the power of appearing to do something.

With that warning in mind, let's turn to consequences. A key consequence of shifting strategy is the unlearning that must be done to effect the shift. This unlearning is probably hardest shifting from being a pioneer than from being a hedger, and probably easiest for a pouncer. For example, as discussed in the prior chapter, hedgers sometimes have difficulty divesting options they should no longer pursue. If the divestment is not made, the learning that occurred from it can act as a drag on firm movement to a new strategy. In the case of pioneers depending on time-pacing and pouncers relying on hyper-competition, that drag can be a significant source of internal friction that dooms the new strategy.

Apart from unlearning, there are other consequences to shifting strategy. One is organizational inertia or friction caused by structures set up to operate under one strategy and now having to cope with a switch. The web of relations existing inside and outside your firm can cause a significant slowdown in execution if not outright adherence to old ways. Alternatively, the problem can be business unit structures not overlapping correctly to execute the new strategy or conflicts preventing the sharing of resources needed by other units under the new strategy.

Also, your firm's momentum can become difficult to change for behavioral reasons. As you should expect, repetitive organizational actions can lead to ingrained behaviors by your personnel. The less thought required to execute daily tasks, or the more frequently those tasks are performed, the more likely perceptions of firm needs will disconnect from actual behavior. For example, your management and personnel can be perfectly aligned on the need for change, and even aligned in thought behind a new strategy. However, the actions required by switching to the new strategy are not aligned because behavior has not changed.

In addition to organizational and behavioral inertia there can be mental inertia as well. Just as repetition of certain activities can cause behavior to mismatch with a new strategy, so too can certain mental repetition cause mismatch between strategies. Your people operating under one strategy may develop shorthand mental procedures that create a framework for how they process incoming information. These mental models, as Peter Senge calls them, can create serious errors when filtering incoming information. Key environmental signals may be missed because your people are inadvertently still operating under the mental frameworks of the old strategy. Unfortunately, the opposite can be true as well. Your people may search for the wrong information or misinterpret its importance (over-rating it, for example). These mental errors can in many ways be more difficult to solve than organizational inertia. And so many leaders don't really address the problem. They announce their strategy once – if at all – and then settle down to the age old solution of reorganizing the firm.

Final Thoughts

By that last comment you probably realize that reorganizing you firm is probably not the single most important management action you can undertake when selecting a pioneer, pouncer, or hedging strategy, or even switching between them. So what actions are important to take? As we wrap up our time together, let me leave you with four key management items that will help ensure your success. They are creating transparency (among your management team), communicating repeatedly (with your staff), delineating important tasks, and finally, setting the appropriate incentive plans.

On transparency, you are not necessarily striving to make the strategy transparent throughout the firm. That could lead to loss of competitive information. Rather, what you want to do is make all critical knowledge transparent to your management team so that they can remove obstacles to progress. What do I mean by critical knowledge? I mean the beliefs that people hold – and act upon – based on what they think they know. This is often called tacit knowledge, and it can compete with explicit knowledge. You see this when you see old behaviors in the face of newly instituted processes. Normally, tacit and explicit knowledge interact to create culture and accompanying behaviors that underpin firm activity in the marketplace. In the face of uncertainty, however, this competition can be anywhere from distracting to downright dangerous to your firm. What this means in terms of promoting transparency is that you must surface such tacit knowledge and make it explicit so that your team can compare it to the explicit knowledge and behavior required to make your chosen strategy a success. Creating such transparency may seem a daunting task on top of actually selecting and timing the right strategy. It may even seem secondary. It isn't. You should understand that only by creating transparency can you forge proper alignment within the firm and execute with less friction.

As for communication, try to convey your strategy – or its key thematic messages – to your employees on a quarterly basis. You'll know you're achieving success when you can stop the random employee in the hallways and you hear back what you want them to understand. Next, communicate to your management team what explicit behaviors you want going forward and what tacit and explicit behaviors you need stopped. When your managers can communicate back to you the relevant behaviors for their respective units, you will know that you have succeeded.

Next, delineate the tasks that will elicit the behaviors you want. I don't mean you should do so personally. But sit down with all your managers and get them to lay out what tasks they will stop doing, tasks they will change how they do them, and new tasks they will take on. Make sure your folks can tie those tasks to behaviors they want to see, or even better, have stopped. You likely will need a consultant to help you make the tie between behaviors, beliefs, and tasks, either old or new. If you have had the helm of your firm for a long time, then you may not know what the new behaviors are that you want, what tasks will elicit them, and how to eliminate the old ones. If you are new to your firm, then the opposite is likely true. You probably do not know what the ties are between the old tasks and beliefs, even if you know what the new ones are that you need. Knowing one and not the other won't help you much. So consider finding a good industrial psychologist consulting group to help you through this key management action.

Finally, incentivize your employees to engage in the new tasks and behaviors to help them shed the old. Like the Sprint example from the prior chapter, set compensation structures that reward your employees for doing the new tasks (right), and don't reward them for repeating old behaviors. Reward those who sacrifice for the greater good. Punish failure carefully, if at all. In other words, follow Edison's tolerance for fault. Allow your good people to learn.

Do these things and do them well, and you will build a firm strong enough to survive the inevitable mistake, strong enough to create its own advantages, and strong enough to master uncertainty.

FURTHER READING

The amount of academic and business literature that has been written on the topics covered in each of the chapters in this book is voluminous and at times daunting. Unfortunately, in keeping with academia's tendency for over-specialization, much of it is either too narrowly focused or overly theoretical. For those of you interested in exploring strategy under uncertainty in further detail, I have highlighted here a half dozen key articles or books that you can use to delve into each of the chapter topics in further detail. Some are "classics," while others are non-technical and more easily accessible to the general reader. The list that follows should provide several helpful starting points if you seek to develop greater knowledge on strategy for mastering uncertainty.

On creating advantage, including the roles of time and capabilities-building:

Collis, David and Cynthia Montgomery. "Competing on Resources: Strategy in the 1990's." Harvard Business Review (Jul-Aug 1995): 108-128.

D'Aveni, Richard. Hyper-Competition: Managing the Dynamics of Strategic Maneuvering. New York: Free Press, 1994.

Eisenhardt, Kathleen and Shona Brown. "Time-pacing - Competing in Markets That Won't Stand Still." Harvard Business Review (Mar-Apr 1998): 59-69.

Stalk, George, Philip Evans, and Lawrence Schulman. "Competing on Capabilities: The New rules of Corporate Strategy." Harvard Business Review (Mar-Apr, 1992): 57-69.

Stalk, George. "Time: The Next Source of Competitive Advantage." Harvard Business Review (Jul-Aug 1988): 41-51.

Yoffie, David and Michael Cusumano. "Judo Strategy - The Competitive Dynamics of Internet Time." Harvard Business Review (Jan-Feb 1999): 71-81.

On pioneering strategy:

Boulding, William and Markus Christen. "First Mover Disadvantage." Harvard Business Review 79 (Oct 2001): 20-21.

Kerin, Roger and Rajan Varadarajan. "First Mover Advantage: A Synthesis, Conceptual Framework, and Research Propositions." Journal of Marketing 56 (Oct 1992): 33-52.

Makadok, Richard. "Can First Mover and Early Mover Advantages Be Sustained in an Industry with Low barriers to Entry-Imitation?." Strategic Management Journal 19 (1998): 683-696.

Mallahi, Kamel and Michael Johnson. "Does it Pay to be a First Mover in e-Commerce? The Case of Amazon." Management Decision 38 (2000): 445-452.

Robinson, William and Sungwook Min. "Is the First to Market the First to Fail? Empirical Evidence for Industrial Goods Businesses." Journal of Marketing Research 34 (Feb 2002): 120-128.

Schnaars, Steven. "When Entering Growth Markets, Are Pioneers Better Than Poachers?." Business Horizons (Mar-Apr 1986): 27-36.

On pouncer strategy:

Bartlett, Christopher and Sumantra Ghoshal. "Going Global: Lessons from Late Movers." Harvard Business Review 78 (Mar-Apr 2000): 132-141.

Carpenter, Gregory and Kent Nakamoto. "Competitive Strategies for Late Entry Into a Market with a Dominant Brand." Management Science 36 (Oct 1990): 1268-1278.

Hoppe, Heidrun and Ulrich Lehmann-Grube. "Second Mover Advantages in Dynamic Quality

Competition." Journal of Economics and Management Strategy 10 (Fall 2001): 419-433.

Lee, Hun, Ken Smith, Curtis Grimm, and August Schomburg. "Timing, Order and Durability of New Product Advantages with Imitation." Strategic Management Journal 21 (2000): 23-30.

Shankar, Venkatesh and Gregory Carpenter. "Late Mover Advantage: How Innovative Late Entrants Outsell Pioneers." Journal of Marketing Research 35 (Feb 1998): 54-70.

On hedging strategy, including the role of real options:

Boer, Peter. "Valuation of Technology Using Real Options." Research Technology Management 43 (Jul-Aug 2000): 26-30.

Copeland, Thomas and Philip Keenan. "Making Real Options Real." McKinsey Quar. 3 (1998): 128-161.

Dixit, Avinash and Robert Pindyck. "The Options Approach to Capital Investment." Harvard Business Review (May-Jun 1995):105-115.

Houldridge, David. "Adopting Real Options as an Accessible and User Friendly Tool Within Your Organization." 4th Annual Conference on Real Options (June 22, 2000).

Luehrman, Timothy. "Strategy as a Portfolio of Real Options." Harvard Business Review (Sep-Oct 1998): 89-99.

Raynor, Michael. "Real Organizations for Real Options: The Administrative Implications of Creating and Exercising Real Options Through Corporate Diversification." 4th Annual Conference on Real Options (Jun 2000).

Trigeorgis, Lenos. "Real Options: An Overview." In Real Options in Capital Investment: Models, Strategies and Applications edited by Lenos Trigeorgis. Westport, CT: Praeger, 1995.

CONCEPTUAL MAP
Developing Your Strategy For Mastering Uncertainty

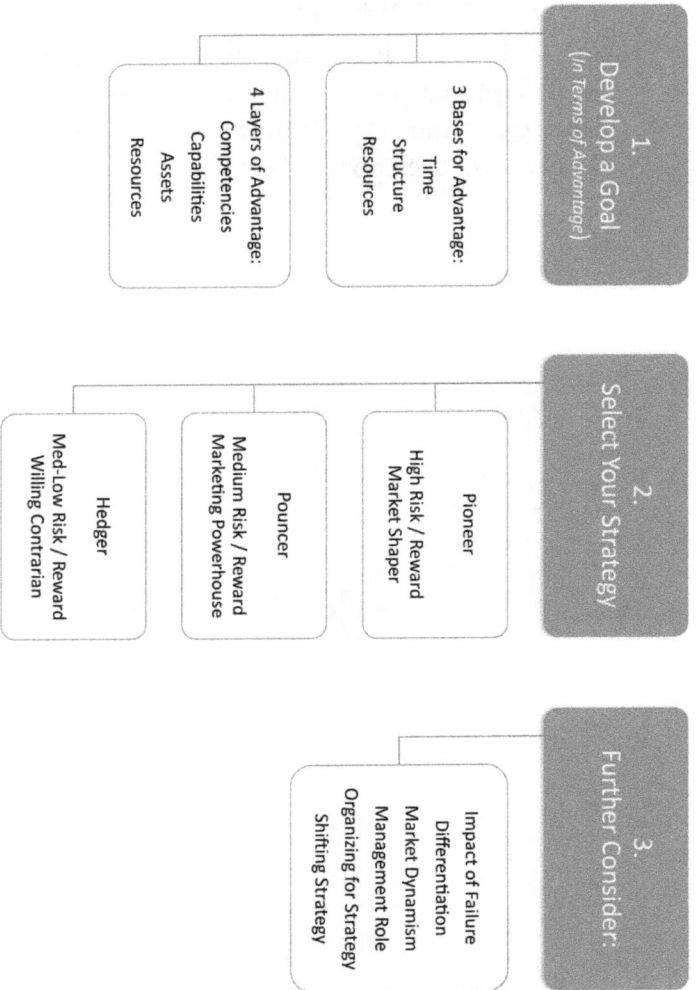

1. Develop a Goal *(In Terms of Advantage)*

- **3 Bases for Advantage:**
  - Time
  - Structure
  - Resources

- **4 Layers of Advantage:**
  - Competencies
  - Capabilities
  - Assets
  - Resources

2. Select Your Strategy

- **Pioneer**
  - High Risk / Reward
  - Market Shaper

- **Pouncer**
  - Medium Risk / Reward
  - Marketing Powerhouse

- **Hedger**
  - Med-Low Risk / Reward
  - Willing Contrarian

3. Further Consider:

- Impact of Failure
- Differentiation
- Market Dynamism
- Management Role
- Organizing for Strategy
- Shifting Strategy

ACKNOWLEDGMENTS

The genesis of this work came out of a series of discussions with one of America's premier strategists, Andrew Marshall, who expressed concern about the absence of rigorous thinking regarding how to manage organizations struggling through periods of uncertainty. My good friends and colleagues Jan van Tol and Andrew May read early versions of this work and provided me invaluable feedback, with special thanks to Bob Boelter for his heroic effort trying to keep me intellectually and verbally crisp and clear. Daniel Levinthal at Wharton and Andrew Sellgren at McKinsey provided useful advice in brief sounding-board sessions when I was at critical junctures in my thinking.

This work could not have happened without the generous assistance of three key institutions. The Smith Richardson Foundation provided financial support during the research phases of the project. Marin Strmecki and Nadia Schadlow guided me through the process, and I owe them deeply for their patronage and their patience with me through the original development phase. The Office of Net Assessment / Office of the Secretary of Defense also provided financial and intellectual support, particularly for the preparation of the outline of an earlier version of this work. The Foreign Policy Institute (FPI) at the Johns Hopkins University Nitze School of Advanced International Studies (SAIS) provided me with a place to research and gave me access to research resources that would have been far harder to obtain otherwise. I specifically would like to thank Drs. Eliot Cohen and Tom Keaney for their patronage while I was a Fellow at the FPI. I would be remiss if I neglected the wonderful SAIS Library staff who helped me track down resources while I was busy researching.

Of course, I owe my biggest debt of gratitude to those who provided me at their own expense the most precious commodities of all – the time to research and write this book and the love and support to help me see it through. My wonderful wife Suzan bore our daughter while I was writing my first book and then my son during this one. All three of them gave up play time so I could begin and complete this project. It is only fair, then, that I now turn my attention to the best part of family life – playtime!

ABOUT THE AUTHOR

Keith Bickel is a business executive and strategist living in the Washington, DC area. His more than two decades of experience span the public, private, and non-profit sectors, including Fortune 50 companies, technology start-ups, the White House Office of Management and Budget, the Office of the Secretary of Defense, and the World Bank. He has particular expertise in leading venture start-ups and building strategy functions – from data-informed market research and competitive intelligence to strategic communications with Boards of Directors.

Dr. Bickel is a frequent speaker on strategy, mortgage markets, and technology issues before select audiences. He has published widely over the years, having written a book on Marine Corps counter-insurgency strategy, Op Eds for various media outlets, and reviews for peer-reviewed journals and grant-making institutions. Among his proudest accomplishments, however, are coaching his two kids to black belts in the martial art of Taekwondo (in which he holds a second degree black belt).

Dr. Bickel graduated with Honors in History and a minor in Neuropsychology from the University of Pennsylvania, and holds both a Masters in International Economics and a Ph.D. in Strategic Studies from the Johns Hopkins Nitze School of Advanced International Studies.